Florida's Fairways

UNIVERSITY PRESS OF FLORIDA

Florida A&M University, Tallahassee
Florida Atlantic University, Boca Raton
Florida Gulf Coast University, Ft. Myers
Florida International University, Miami
Florida State University, Tallahassee
University of Central Florida, Orlando
University of Florida, Gainesville
University of North Florida, Jacksonville
University of South Florida, Tampa
University of West Florida, Pensacola

Florida's

University Press of Florida
Gainesville · Tallahassee · Tampa · Boca Raton
Pensacola · Orlando · Miami · Jacksonville · Ft. Myers

Fairways

60 Alluring and Affordable Golf Courses
from the Panhandle to the Keys

Alan K. Moore

Copyright 2006 by Alan K. Moore
Printed in Canada on recycled, acid-free paper
All rights reserved

11 10 09 08 07 06   6 5 4 3 2 1

Library of Congress Cataloging-in-Publication Data
Moore, Alan K.
Florida's fairways: 60 alluring and affordable golf courses from the
panhandle to the Keys / Alan K. Moore.
p. cm.
Includes bibliographical references.
ISBN 0-8130-3021-8 (alk. paper)
1. Golf courses—Florida—Guidebooks.
2. Golf courses—Florida—Directories. I. Title.
GV982.F5M66   2006
796.352'068759—dc22   2006022028

The University Press of Florida is the scholarly publishing agency
for the State University System of Florida, comprising Florida A&M
University, Florida Atlantic University, Florida Gulf Coast University,
Florida International University, Florida State University, University
of Central Florida, University of Florida, University of North Florida,
University of South Florida, and University of West Florida.

University Press of Florida
15 Northwest 15th Street
Gainesville, FL 32611-2079
http://www.upf.com

To those who keep the land for golf

Contents

Part III. Tampa Area and Gulf Coast

Part IV. Atlantic Coast to Key West

Preface

Sitting in an Orlando hotel room, I pulled the Gideon Bible from the bedside drawer and opened it at random. Glaring like a beacon were the words "Take a stick and write on it" (Ezek. 37:16). Having just discussed with my editor the possibility of writing a golf guide to the state, I saw a clear message. I'm not suggesting this was a God-given task, although it did feel divine to experience so many courses in this golf-centric state.

Florida is the golf capital of America. More than two million golfers visit the state every year. Eleven hundred public courses entice tourists from across North America and Europe, in particular Great Britain and Ireland. Many purchase golf packages. Snowbirds spend their winter days with club in hand.

Professional golfers populate the state as movie stars do Hollywood. Several prestigious tournaments offer chances to see them in action: the annual Tournament Players Championship at Sawgrass, Arnold Palmer's tournament at Bay Hill, the Honda Classic at PGA National, and the World Golf Championship at Doral. Events on the Champions (Seniors) Tour, LPGA Tour, and minitours ensure Florida a busy play-for-pay status.

Many golf associations and enterprises are located in the state. The PGA Tour headquarters is in Ponte Vedra, the LPGA in Daytona Beach. The PGA of America is based in Palm Beach Gardens, and the Golf Channel in Orlando.

This selection of Florida's courses will highlight the variety of architects who have trimmed and pruned Nature to reveal the holes lying in wait beneath her skirts. No favoritism is intended. My choice is partly based on geography, wanting to cover the map but with the obvious central and coastal weighting.

I believe these are sixty of the best and most accessible public courses the state has to offer. Initially I chose a core of courses for inclusion; others I stumbled upon, as might an independent golfing traveler. A few were personally recommended by players, professionals, and course architects.

Some higher-fee courses and resorts are included in order to cater for all budgets. During research in 2005, no course had immediate plans to turn private, though a handful hinted that this might be a long-term possibility.

My intent in writing this book is to guide you to courses where you can experience a pleasurable round of golf, admire the flora and fauna along the way, and maintain a peaceful frame of mind.

Green Fee

The green fee listed includes golf cart and should be the maximum you have to pay. Prices are based on the 2006 winter season, January through March. The fee shown is for a weekend before noon. (Fees are usually lower on weekdays and after 1 or 2 p.m. on any day; they are even lower at twilight.) Summer green fees tend to be half the winter price. Other seasonal variances occur; some discounted rates apply for local and state residents. Please check with individual courses for the rate applicable to your visit.

Club Rental

Expect the average rental fee for clubs to be around $20 per set; the higher the green fee, the higher the rental. At one club the green fee was $50 and $15 rented top-of-the-line clubs. At another, I paid $60 for golf and $20 for club rental and was given a mixed bag with no sand wedge. Do not expect shoe rental at these courses, though Orange County National and Miami Beach offer this service.

Practice Facilities

All clubs in this guide have at least a driving range and practice putting area, save the following:

Hilaman Park: irons-only driving range
Mount Dora: short-game practice area
Lekarica: irons-only driving range
The Claw: irons-only driving range
River Run: short-game practice area
Colony West: adjoining par-3 course
Key West: large practice net

Dress

Clothes maketh the man. Any golfer beyond the first weeks of addiction will have gathered that the dress standard is chinos or tailored shorts, and collared shirt. Call me old fogey if you will, but I would never dream of telling a lady how to dress.

Climate

Florida's warm climate is world renowned. A few nights during winter the temperature may fall to freezing point. Early mornings can be cool, so a windbreaker comes in handy. Summer brings humidity and scattered rain. Courses have signs alerting players to the possibility of lightning. Hurricane season officially begins in June and peaks in September; some years none arrive, in other years they overwhelm. Protection from harmful rays of the sun is advised always; wear sunscreen.

Critters

When told what to expect from Florida's wildlife, I was worried about a constant threat from alligators. I saw fewer than a dozen on my journeys around the state, although anywhere with more than a standing pond of casual water admits to their presence. Crocodiles live in the mangroves around Key Biscayne. Snakes are more prevalent, and prove the best incentive for hitting straight, since hunting for balls in the undergrowth is not encouraged. In protected wetlands it is forbidden. Squirrels, rabbits, and tortoises are more visible, plus the odd fox. The beauty of Florida wildlife lies in its bird population. Every day is a spectacle. Expect to see ibis, sandhill cranes, wood storks, herons, pelicans, cormorants, anhingas, egrets, hawks, and eagles. From a day on Longboat Key, Sarasota, my notes read "Hole #13 ROSEATE SPOONBILL!!!" Florida's golf courses are truly an aviary of exotica.

Walking the Course

If permitted at all, walking is allowed most afternoons (except weekends in winter high season) and on some back nines in the early morning. A number of courses allow walking at any time. This book is not meant to be specifically a walking guide. The advent of the golf cart has added a major source of revenue for the golf industry. Be aware: if you choose to walk, some clubs charge the cart fee anyway. Cart paths are here to stay, but golf courses were here first. Although the concrete thread winding through our golfscapes is the yellow brick road to our kingdom of Oz, let us never lose sight of the kingdom of Fife.

Yardage, Course Ratings, and Slope Ratings

Professional events are staged on courses around 7,000 yards long. For the average golfer, studies have shown an optimum 6,400 yards for men, 5,800 yards for women, and 6,224 yards for male seniors. Throughout this guide I list lengths played from blue tees and red tees or their equivalent. The extreme player can usually find a more challenging set; happy hackers can be sure a set of tees exists more suited to their ability.

Course rating is a way to assess the difficulty of a course. The figure is expressed to one decimal place, and indicates what a scratch golfer should expect to score. If scorecard par is 72 and the course rating is 68.1, the player knows it is an easier track; if the course rating is 74.6, then it's tougher. The number, assigned by the USGA, is usually within a couple strokes of par. Europeans have a similar system called Standard Scratch Score.

Slope rating is also determined by the USGA and tells high handicappers the difficulty of the golf course. The scale ranges from 55 (an easy nine holes) to 155 (a tough eighteen). A course with a slope rating of 115 is of average difficulty.

In analysis of holes, I describe play from the blue tees with a drive of anything from 200 to 250 yards, and a 5-iron second shot, or approach, between 150 and 175 yards. I have found that most landing area hazards are within that range.

Driving Directions

All mileages from an interstate highway are measured from the center to compensate for north/southbound or east/westbound exit differentials. They should be accurate to within one-tenth of a mile. Route numbers are given priority; familiar road names are listed in parentheses. In the event of a road having two numerical identities—where, for example, routes 44 West and 47 North share tarmac—the first is given preference and its twin printed thus: [47 North].

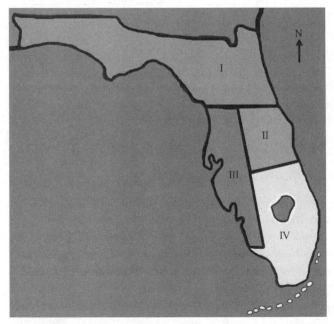

Florida's Regions in This Guide

Acknowledgments

My thanks are due to all the professionals and staff at the courses listed in this book, especially to the following for help, advice, information, time, and a few friendships forged along the way:

Dan Hagar (Boynton Beach), Chris Eckart (Sandridge), Alex Romanoff (The Habitat), Sandra Eriksson and Bill Kriews (Delray Beach), Deb Hurd (PGA National), Stephen Cox (Okeeheelee), Randy Weber (Miami Beach), Kevin C. Smith (Department of Parks and Recreation, City of Miami Beach), Christopher Gamble (Fairwinds), Toby Sherman (Colony West), Jim Torba (ex Miami Beach), Susan Walker (Palmetto), Karen Campbell (Crandon), Bob Loring (Pompano Beach), Gabrielle Rothman (The Biltmore), Bruce K. Harwood II (Stoneybrook), Marsha Harris (Coral Oaks), Scott Wyckoff (World Woods), Jim Crocci (The Dunes), Rick Roberts (El Diablo), Dave Stewart (Fox Hollow), Jim Fee (The Claw at USF), Clint Wright (River Run), Chad Robertson and Jason Dewildt (Orange County National), Marion Walker (Highlands Reserve), Jeff Parsons (Diamondback), Shane Trice and Ralph Forrest (Southern Dunes), Kenny Winn and Fabian McIntyre (Falcon's Fire), Paul Fisher (MetroWest), Brady Godfrey (Harbor Hills), Brooks Barth and David "Cotton" Smith (Mount Dora), Clark Creamer (Ocala), Mike Doucette and Jeff Peterson (DeBary), David Buth and Matt Payne (Victoria Hills), Randy Sansing (Cleveland Heights), Rafe Kirian and Rob Morton (Black Bear), Chris Conlon and Erik Anderson (Wekiva), Jim Wright (Marcus Pointe), Scott Sandler (Hilaman Park), Ron Brooks and Harold Hoover (Southern Oaks), Bob Geppert and Ryan Phelps (Bent Creek), Chris Blocker, Billy Maxwell, and Gary Murfitt (Hyde Park), Jay Jameson (Cypress Head), Bill Iwinski (Ironwood), Jamie Ledvina (Meadowbrook), Chris Brandt (Lake Jovita); Greg Bare at Dubsdread, Jim Ward at Pointe West, and Gary Crothers at Montague, Vermont.

Glenn Nowicki and Heather Wrede allowed me to invade their home. Jim Schleutcher gave me a basic knowledge of turfgrass science. Jim Kennedy and Bill Below aided in course selection.

Ron Garl, Ricky Nix, David W. Gordon, Bruce Devlin, Roger Rulewich, and Mike Dasher were all kind enough to give of their time. Roy Case set the ball rolling.

Meredith Morris-Babb and John Byram at the University Press of Florida took up the idea and saw it through to completion with patience. Copy editor Ann Marlowe and project editor Michele Fiyak-Burkley provided first-rate editorial suggestions and support.

Part I

North Florida

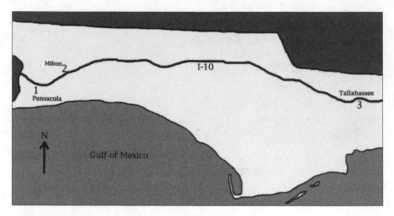

The Panhandle and Tallahassee

1   Marcus Pointe
2   The Moors
3   Hilaman Park

Marcus Pointe

2500 Oak Pointe Drive, Pensacola 32505
(850) 484-9770
www.marcuspointe.com

Green fee: $49

Architect: Earl Stone, 1990
Par 72
Blue yardage 6,225; course rating 69.8; slope rating 123
Red yardage 5,185; course rating 69.7; slope rating 121

*Directions: From I-10 exit 10, go south on 29 (Pensacola Boulevard) 1.3 miles.
At 453 (W Street) turn right, go 0.4 miles to Marcus Pointe Boulevard, and
turn right again. In 1.0 miles, at Oak Pointe Drive, turn left; entrance is ahead.*

Up and running after Ivan.

Looking back up the valley fairway on eight.

Hurricane Ivan devastated the Caribbean island of Grenada in September 2004, leaving 94 percent of the population homeless. Ivan continued north to wreak havoc in Jamaica and was one of four destructive hurricanes to torment Florida that year. It came ashore at Pensacola the day I received the go-ahead to write this book. With a suspicion my writing was cosmically challenged, I counted my blessings. I still had a roof over my head, clothes on my back, and food in my belly. After Ivan and Charlie and Frances and Jeanne, Florida and its folk were suffering.

I had wanted to cover Florida from tip to toe. Unfortunately, the tip was one of the areas hardest hit. Lost Key was indeed lost and is, as I write nineteen months later, about to reopen. But Marcus Pointe, where Ivan felled five hundred trees, was soon up and running for golf.

Built on the site of an old paper mill, Marcus Pointe has a surprisingly timeless look and pleasing variety in elevation. Six holes rise (a couple in cardiac grade), six fall, and the others run fairly flat. Half the holes dogleg, and oaks and pines border fairways on both sides. Water is a lateral hazard on a couple of occasions and, of forty-odd bunkers, most are placed greenside. An attractive corridor shared by the first and ninth holes, and perimeter holes ten and eleven, suggest the design's starting points. Width is given for the recreational golfer, an appreciation that our drives are often wayward. Architect Earl Stone knows who pays the money and that the majority don't play from the longer, gold tees. Yet from these, at 6,736 yards, it can be a tricky track. Once a venue for the Hogan Tour, it also hosted the Monday Qualifier for the former Blue Angels Classic at The Moors.

Number one measures 400 yards and is rated hardest hole on this side. The fairway angles right at the 150-yard marker; the ground also tilts that way. Two bunkers guard the L-shaped green. The second fairway is narrow and cupped, with an oak standing out from the right-hand tree line 160 yards from the target. The elevated green is deep and slopes from the rear. A 141-yard one-shot follows.

The fourth drifts downhill, widening as it progresses. The kidney-shaped putting surface has a crown at the inner curve and sheds outwards. Bunkers squeeze the entrance at both sides. Five continues downhill through a narrow chute, then slides left around a large oak 180 yards from the green. From 110 yards out, the fairway breaks into mounds and swales. A front bunker forces an aerial approach to the flag, and a pond off to the right drags the land in that direction.

Six plays uphill 144 yards. A cloverleaf bunker at front left mirrors the shape of the green; two round shallow bunkers sit center right. The eighth runs downhill into a valley, with mounding heavier to the left as a barrier for housing. A fairway bunker sits 125 yards out from the elevated green, guarded on the right by two others.

The ninth is a par 5 of 480 yards and elbows slightly left at the halfway mark. Two single oaks encroach upon the fairway at the turning point, from where the approach climbs steadily to the green complex. Free-form bunkers surround the deep three-tier putting surface.

The back nine begins with a downhill of 326 yards, drivable for today's strong players. Bunkers cover the green front, so a layup might prove the wiser option. The target is wide but shallow, and falls off at the rear.

Eleven, a 464-yard par 5, shoots sharply uphill to a right-angled dogleg, where a bunker waits at the inner corner 200 yards from the hole. The right side gives the best approach position. A four-lobed bunker guards the front left of an elongated three-lobed green. Flashed hazards sit to the rear and center right. Twelve lies spoonlike inside eleven, doglegging left and downhill. The second shot gives a panoramic view over the green to the hundred-acre lake that winds around Marcus Pointe.

The fourteenth is rated hardest hole, a 415-yard dogleg left and uphill. Water runs to the right off the tee. Bunkers wait at the right side of the landing area. The fairway falls away to the right; hitting left seems the only way of getting good position. A solitary oak sits 60 yards off the green—to the right, of course.

A sign en route to the next tee proclaims this Gilbert's Corner. A steep descent to a wooden boardwalk over the lake allows carts to reach roller-coaster speed. Gilbert Nelson was zipping down the hill when he noticed another cart parked at the entrance to the boardwalk, the occupant attending to a call of nature in the nearby bushes. Gilbert and his cart had nowhere else to go and plunged into the water.

Fifteen runs through a narrow chute off the tee and doglegs doubly. Water sits off to the right from the 100-yard marker, and high ground takes the left side, continuing with greenside mounds containing a pair of pot bunkers. The seventeenth is a 175-yard one-shot to a teardrop green, with three pots guarding the front. The putting surface slopes to the front left quarter.

A dogleg left draws the round to a close. A bunker sits at the inner angle, 175 yards from the target. The ground rises to a forward-sloping green, guarded by white sand pots at left and a yellow sand cape bunker on the right.

Head professional Jim Wright was very amenable to helping me start off my Florida golfing trail. He whispered that some folks call this area LA, meaning Lower Alabama. Himself a native of that state, he informed me that course architect Earl Stone was born in Florida, but most of his work is in Alabama. A fair exchange if ever there was one.

The Moors Golf and Lodging

3220 Avalon Boulevard, Milton 32583
(850) 995-4653
www.moors.com

Green fee: $59

Architect: John LaFoy, 1993
Par 70
Blue yardage 6,443; course rating 71.2; slope rating 125
Red yardage 5,259; course rating 70.3; slope rating 117

*Directions: From I-10 exit 22, go north on 281 (Avalon Boulevard) 1.3 miles;
entrance is on right.*

Home of the former Blue Angels Classic.

Hand mowing the third, a replica of Troon's Postage Stamp.

Sidney Lee sold groceries from his store in Birmingham, Alabama. Together with a chemist, he concocted Buffalo Rock Ginger Ale. By 1927 the drink was so successful that he branched out into soda distribution throughout the South. Buffalo Rock is now the nation's largest privately owned bottler and distributor of Pepsi-Cola. Jim C. Lee III, great-grandson of the founder, wanted to give something back to the communities that helped build the family fortune. A golf enthusiast already operating one course, Bent Brook, in Birmingham, he decided to build another in Florida and determined to keep it open to the public.

He purchased an old dairy farm near Milton, and work began. Lying below sea level, the land had to be raised by three feet. Much imported dirt and shaping left an enormous field of giant moguls. Nearly every mound is topped with a clump or two of native grasses. Few trees stand within the course, giving rise to the modern (erroneous) golf logic: No trees = Scottish links. Neither is the Moors a watercourse, although *aqua reclamata* does come into play on eight holes. The routing is arranged in a core design, with homes bordering early holes on the back nine.

For eleven years the Moors was the home of the Blue Angels Classic, an official Champions Tour event held every May. Seventy senior professionals battled it out over three days near the white beaches of Pensacola. This was the only PGA event with military backing, the Blue Angels being the U.S. Navy's acrobatic flying squadron. Although the tournament was not directly sponsored by the Department of Defense, the profits went to the Naval Aviation Museum Foundation and other charities. In 2006 the event became the Boeing Championship and moved to Destin.

It's not a long course played from the blue tees—one par 5 on each side makes par 70. This is about the number of bunkers, all conventional shapes, pots and ovals, a few placed 15 to 25 yards off greens. The Moors is not a roller coaster ride but a good workday at the golfing office. If it's grand enough for senior professionals, then it's good enough for the average golfer. An eight-room pension attached to the clubhouse lends guests a feeling of exclusivity.

Beginning with a dogleg left, water lies to the right on the approach. Two pot bunkers, one on each side, sit 15 yards off the green front. Two more lie by the green. The second hole plays back to the clubhouse, sliding right this time. Drives from the tiny, round tee boxes may encounter pot bunkers placed near the 150-yard marker at left. The formation is mirrored greenside: three hazards left and one right.

The third is a replica of Troon's Postage Stamp, albeit more than 50 yards longer than the 126-yard original. Mounds stand to the left, and bunkers encircle the green. An especially nasty "sucker" pot bunker sits front right. At the 395-yard fifth, a lake frames the left side all the way. The fairway narrows into the green, which tilts to the right.

Six is rated hardest hole at the Moors, doglegging left around a lake. Bunkers cover the inner angle, and trees line the right. The green pitches forward and is guarded in front by sand hazards in a two-left, one-right combination.

The seventh fairway has ample landing area but is bunkered to the right side. Three pine trees cover the right-hand line to the target on this par 5; water discourages attempts to hook around them. The safe play bails out left for a shorter approach. A crown at center right dominates the breaks on this elevated green.

Nine's 443 yards undulate until interrupted by swamp at wedge distance. The green is mounded behind, and a bunker lies rear right. The 528-yard eleventh is the long hole on the back nine. Three spreading oaks stand by the 250-yard marker, and cross bunkers cover the right approach 140 yards from the green. Hazards lie greenside left, and the front half of the green slopes forward.

Twelve measures 181 yards with chocolate-drop mounds occupying the fairway. A big bunker covers the front left, and two more sit behind the wide green, sloping predominantly to the right.

The next three are similar in length, averaging 375 yards, and of medium difficulty. Number thirteen forces a carry over water from the tee and angles left to an unguarded cornflake green. The fourteenth has bunkers on both sides of the landing area and hazards at greenside. On fifteen, a bunker cluster sits right of the 150-yard marker, but the ground drops away to the right beyond. The green is guarded front and rear on the left side.

Sixteen is a one-shot of 188 yards. Bunkers lie rear left and front right of the forward-sloping green. A pin position at rear right proves a test.

The eighteenth has water to the right, squeezing the fairway at the 150-yard marker, where a cluster of bunkers sits left. Bunkers swarm all over the front of the green, and two wait at the rear.

Purists bemoan the artificiality of modern-day courses, but architects have to be creative with what land is available. In some aspects the Moors is an obviously prepared playing field. Chocolate-drop mounding and the extent of cord and pampas grass make it quite unlike any other course in this region. But, again, if it was good enough for the Champions Tour . . .

3

Hilaman Park

2737 Blair Stone Road, Tallahassee 32301
(850) 891-3935
www.talgov.com/parks/hilmgolf.cfm

Green fee: $35

Architects: Edward Lawrence Packard and Roger Packard, 1972
Par 72
Blue yardage 6,333; course rating 70.5; slope rating 123
Red yardage 5,400; course rating 71.5; slope rating 121

*Directions: From I-10 exit 199, drive south on 27 (Monroe Street) 4.0 miles. At
27 East (Apalachee Parkway) turn left. Go 1.9 miles to 373 (Blair Stone Road)
and turn right. In 1.0 miles, entrance is on left.*

Edward Lawrence Packard's sixty-three holes at Innisbrook Resort in Tarpon
Springs are considered among his finest works. The fact that he retired there
in the mid-1980s indicates he accorded them similar value. Alas, Innisbrook
restricts play to resort guests, though bona fide members of other clubs can
arrange to play there with a letter of introduction. One of Packard's courses the
keen student of golf architecture can play year round is Hilaman Park, located
within three miles of the State Capitol building in Tallahassee.

This is a perfect example of the architectural style known as English Parks—
set in rolling landscape with mature trees (see color plate 1). Holes are paired
in shared corridors with significant changes in elevation. Downhill on one hole
means uphill on the next. The corridor shared by thirteen and fourteen follows
this gradient to the most striking extent. The front nine loops north, the back
nine to the south. The course is light on bunkers, about thirty, with the majority
placed greenside in regular oval and cape shapes. There are no tricks or visual
effects to perturb the player. This is a strong municipal facility that other cities
on the peninsula must envy.

Hilaman Park was built as a private club, Winewood. The wine was too
heady, obviously, since it closed in 1981 and was sold to the city for around $10
million. Sheldon "Shad" Hilaman was mayor and city commissioner in 1981

Swing correction.

when he died in office. It is a fitting tribute to this public servant that the course reopened under his name the following year.

The opening hole runs gently downhill to a bowl 100 yards from the green. Water lies to the left, and a tree barrier to the right is shared with the second hole. The fairway rises to a green angling left and bunkered in front. Two's approach is uphill, the green guarded front and rear by sand hazards.

The third is a par 5 of 528 yards. One bunker is placed to the right of the first landing area, while another sits 80 yards off the green to the left. The green is well bunkered front and rear and must be one of the closest in the world to a multistory car park! Florida's Department of Corrections administration building is located here, and signs warn us of video surveillance and remind us we are responsible for all golf ball damage. Correct your swing, or you might find yourself a state statistic.

The fourth, a short par 4, plays downhill into a gully. Any drive over 250 yards will end up in a pond fronting the green. It has no other hazards. At the 182-yard fifth, the target is framed by a yellow sand hazard to the right and a white sand bunker left. Pick a color—green is the favorite.

Six winds 490 yards uphill, doglegging to the right. A generous first landing area has a bunker at the outer angle. The way narrows from 100 yards into the unprotected green. The small putting surface feeds into a grass hollow at center right. Seven's fairway, by contrast, is tight, kicking left and downhill steeply from the 150-yard marker. Two deep pots sit greenside right, and one bunker lies left of the forward-sloping green.

Voluminous bunkers surround the green of the 164-yard, par-3 eighth. Nine's tee shot plays uphill into a chute with mounding at left and a large spreading oak 100 yards off the tee to the right. A bunker sits to the left 240 yards from the tee. The approach turns left and is graded a touch downhill to an angled green. A cape bunker covers the left, and two pots sit behind.

The back nine begins with a downhill tee shot favoring a fade. One bunker covers the green front, and a pot guards the rear right. The putting surface steps down from a high tier at the left.

The 405-yard eleventh doglegs left. The further right you are at the 150-yard marker, the better the opening to the green. A fat three-bay bunker guards the left side. Twelve is a penal 154-yard carry over a lake. The green, 40 yards wide, collects into a central funnel. Two rear sand hazards mean pinpoint accuracy is required to hold the shallow target, 15 yards deep.

The thirteenth, a par 5 of 501 yards, calls for one of the few forced carries at Hilaman Park, over wetland to a rising fairway that curves left and continues up, up, and up through the trees. The ever-narrowing fairway ends at the sloping target with a bunker at front right. Fourteen doglegs downhill to the right, and steeply on the approach. Banking to the left takes tee shots around the corner. Two deep frontal traps guard the green, which drops off behind. The putting surface slopes to the front right quarter.

Fifteen has water off the tee to the right side and edges left in a gentle uphill gradient. Sixteen is the last forced carry over water; a rising fairway slides right with trouble in the shape of rough, wetland, and a cavernous bunker sitting at the foot of the green. A bailout area of grass hollows lies to the left and rear of the target.

Seventeen is a 214-yard one-shot with a lone bunker at front left and grass hollows to the right. The home hole has one sand hazard to the right of the landing area. Mature oaks block the gate at the final approach, which has to be grounded or sent sky high. The green needs no further protection.

The course was renovated by Chip Powell in 1999 and has a range for irons only. Hilaman Park hosts the city championship during June, but any month of the year is fine to play in such a beautiful setting at so reasonable a price.

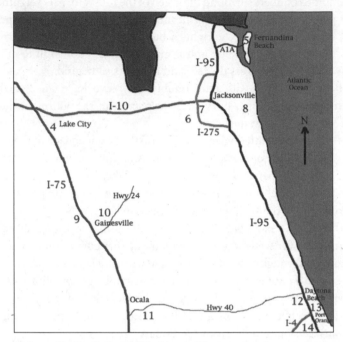

Jacksonville, North Central Florida, and Daytona Beach

  4 Southern Oaks
  5 Fernandina Beach
  6 Bent Creek
  7 Hyde Park
  8 Windsor Parke
  9 Meadowbrook
10 Ironwood
11 Ocala
12 LPGA International
13 Daytona Beach
14 Cypress Head

Southern Oaks Golf Club

717 Northwest Fairway Drive, Lake City 32055
(386) 752-2266

Green fee: $45

Architect: Willard Byrd, 1970
Par 72
Blue yardage 6,364; course rating 70.4; slope rating 129
Gold yardage 5,067; course rating 68.6; slope rating 117

*Directions: From I-75 exit 427, go east on 90 for 0.2 miles. At Commerce
Boulevard turn left. In 1.3 miles, entrance is on right.*

Ron Brooks was raised on a farm fifteen miles from Lake City. He devoted
his business life to cleaning and maintaining surfaces people walk on, namely
carpets. His company cleaned carpets in restaurants all over the South. At
sixty-eight years of age he decided to retire and get himself a golf course. Since
buying the old Lake City Country Club in 2002, he lavishes as much attention
on greens and fairways as he ever did on carpeting. The result is a wonder to
behold. I thought the first putting surface was a new strain of Bermuda hybrid
dwarf grass, it was such a brilliant shade of green. One enthusiast flew three
buddies from West Palm Beach in his own plane just to putt on these greens.

As Ron Brooks is a gentleman of the old school, complete with southern
hospitality and charm, so is the design of Southern Oaks. Willard Byrd concentrated his efforts in Georgia and the Carolinas, though his work also features at
Longboat Key Resort off Sarasota. Three holes at Southern Oaks play around a
lake. A half dozen include stark elevation changes, but the character is mostly
rolling land, tree-lined fairways, and greens with softly pronounced breaks.
Homes are pleasantly set way back from fairway borders.

On the 365-yard first, a wide chute of trees narrows to 25 yards at the 150-
yard marker. The green has one pot bunker to the right and one bunker left.
The par-5 second has a bunker right of the first landing area. The hole then
slides left to a round green with front bunkering. The 414-yard third is straight
and wide, with two bunkers left of the 200-yard marker. The raised green com-

plex includes a front left bunker; water curls around behind from the right side.

The next three holes play around the lake. After hurricanes in 2004, the lake spilled over the protective berm and these holes were submerged for two months. Maintenance staff took to rowboats and paddled around repairing the shoreline.

Four is a par 4 of 337 yards. Apart from the water, a front bunker is the only hazard. Five is a penal par 3, 174 yards carried over the drink. The green has a bulkhead bunker at the water's edge; a conventional sand hazard guards the left. A small hump at back left feeds balls to the right.

Teeing off beside a thick line of oaks and attractive lakeside homes, number six plays to a wide fairway. A bunker lies left at the 150-yard marker. The raised green has deep bunkers at both sides and a vertical gully in the front half of the putting surface.

The seventh takes play away from the lake to higher ground in a 149-yard, par-3 fashion, uphill. The putting surface is not visible from the tee, but a tall magnolia tree behind the green gives a good line. The hazards are two front lobes of sand and a little pot behind.

Three holes play around a lake.

Eleven's green
with fifteen in the
background.

A pond immediately off the tee should present no problem at the eighth. Internal chanting of "It's not there! It's not there!" may help.

The ninth plays downhill through a narrow chute of trees to the first landing area 200 yards from the tee. As the hole doglegs right, a pond at the inner angle prevents longer players trying to cut the corner. The approach rises slightly to a circular green draped by bunkers at the front and a pot to the rear left.

Ten is rated hardest hole, a par 4 of 421 yards. A pond lies to the left at driving distance, 200 to 150 yards from the green; trees block the right side. Dog-legging left and uphill, the approach finds the green protected at both sides by hazards. A semicircle of large oaks once framed the rear of the green, and their shade inhibited the growth of grass. The owner admits that the zealous pruning of arboreal features was initially unpopular. The green surfaces, he says, are what bring people back.

The eleventh measures 521 yards. The fairway kicks left at the 100-yard marker where a long sand feature covers the left-side approach and a row of four pot bunkers punctuates the right. One of the larger greens at Southern Oaks, eleven's measures 8,000 square feet.

Fourteen doglegs right and climbs sharply on the second shot. Bunkers enclose both sides of the angle 110 yards from the target. The two-tier green falls to the front right quarter, spilling into a sand hazard. This is the only green where Common Bermuda grass refused to flourish and was replaced with more resilient Tifdwarf.

Fifteen is a 179-yard one-shot to a punchbowl green. Accuracy is required, as the target is framed by sand on both sides. Sixteen, at 515 yards, spoons around fourteen; thus, the tee shot is downhill to a dogleg-left landing area. Unseen from the tee, a 70-yard pond takes over the fairway from the 200-yard marker. Bunkers lobe the sides of the forward sloping green.

After a one-shot at seventeen, the round finishes with a straight uphill play. Staggered bunkers line the landing area at 150 yards from the green center. A greenside bunker should be the last of your worries.

The Women's Senior Golf Tour has adopted Southern Oaks as home for its annual Qualifying School. I expect Ron Brooks views this as a compliment not to be brushed aside . . . or under the carpet.

Fernandina Beach Golf Club

2800 Bill Melton Road, Fernandina Beach 32034
(904) 277-7370

Green fee: $44

Architects: Ed Matteson, 1956, 1959; Tommy Birdsong, 1972

Blue/Red	North+West	West+South	South+North
Par	72/73	73/73	71/72
Yardage	6,777/5,638	7,001/5,290	6,412/5,100
Course rating	72.0/71.7	73.1/69.4	70.1/68.7
Slope rating	124/118	128/115	124/116

*Directions: From I-95 exit 373, go east on 200 (A1A) 11.3 miles to Amelia
Island Parkway. Turn right, go 2.5 miles to Via Del Ray, and turn left. Entrance
is in 0.4 miles, on left.*

Fernandina Beach prides itself historically on having lived under eight different flags; twenty-seven more fly at the Fernandina Beach Golf Club. If this venue were any farther north it would be in Georgia. In fact, Amelia Island is southernmost in the chain of Golden Isles, which include Jekyll Island and Sea Island. A visit to the local museum located in the old jailhouse reveals the reason for the prevalence of the local name Egmont. The first earl of Egmont helped found Georgia, naming it after his king, George II. John Perceval, second earl of Egmont, named Amelia Island after the king's daughter. Owning 10,000 acres of the island, he established a flourishing indigo plantation, an essential contemporary source for blue dye. The colorful connection was severed by the American Revolution and the handing over of the lands of Florida to Spain.

Situated within walking distance of some fancy neighbors complete with upscale prices, this club is where you come on vacation for a stress-free round without sinking a hole in your bank balance.

The North Course, from 1956 and designed by head professional Ed Matteson, is unpretentious golf on flat land. It plays out and back for six holes, with a tight little loop for last three, the ninth doglegging back to the clubhouse. There

The West Course.

are no great carries or strategic problems to ponder. Greens are small with bunkering typical for the times. One can imagine a television interview from the 1950s with a golfer explaining the game as if to an alien audience: "Well, you have to hit it down the fairway and miss the bunker, if there is one. Then hit again for the green. If you miss, you'll be in one of two traps. When your ball is on the green, you take a couple putts and move to the next hole." I think I speak for the majority when I say we manage to make it a lot more complicated.

The first does feature a bunker to the right, 75 yards from the green, complete with its own island and palm tree. The raised green has bunkers at both sides, just where you'd expect them. The par-5 second continues north with mounded pot bunkers at the first landing area. The green slopes left with two front sand hazards on guard. On the par-3 third, a gully funnels the putting surface from rear left center to the front left quarter.

Four's fairway bunker is left of the 150-yard marker, and two more sit at the green front. Five's fairway bunker lies to the right, 100 yards from the green, with hazards right and rear this time. The 381-yard ninth doglegs left around large, overhanging oaks at the inner angle. The green tilts forward, guarded by a bunker on the right side.

By 1959 the city was ready to unveil another nine holes at the locale. The West Course displays Ed Matteson gaining confidence with his task. With a larger land parcel available, he paired holes in a more pleasing fashion. The first three share a corridor with the final three; four and six share their own plot with the par-5 fifth. Three par 5s give the West 600 yards more length than its older sister.

After a wide opener to a flat green, the second lopes in at 607 yards. The fairway is ample in width, just so very long; it will probably be a regulation two-shot hole by the time this book is published. To the right, away from the solitary greenside bunker, a dense stand of bowing oaks gives the impression of cathedral vaulting. The third green also has a front-right sand defense. The putting surface gathers to the center.

Pine trees frame the right-hand side of the 491-yard fifth off the tee. On the approach, mounded pot bunkers, two left and one right, sit 25 yards from the green, which has its own guardian bunker on the right. Some of us have trouble reaching the 227-yard, par-3 sixth. (Perhaps it's time to move forward to the white tees.)

Seven slides to the right. The green has a bunker to the left and a central gully in the putting surface. The par-3 ninth brings us back to the clubhouse.

Bowing oaks give the impression of cathedral vaulting.

Tommy Birdsong's South Course takes us out into swampy territory. This nine is a shade more muscular. We are now in 1972, and the change is as striking as from black-and-white to Technicolor. Holes dogleg, we have water carries and a major road to contend with, even special signals to warn traffic we wish to cross and continue our round in safety.

The first tee shot is through a very narrow chute of trees and mature magnolias in the fairway. Clearing them leaves 235 yards at this 499-yard par 5. The fairway draws left, with a right bunker at the 150-yard marker. Greenside hazards give a tight opening to a deep, narrow green. Two's tee shot is a penal carry over water to the angle of this dogleg right. Water continues to the right with a saving gully at greenside. The angled green has a bunker at front left.

The fourth is a par 5 of 591 yards. Wide in the first landing area, the hole fades to the right with young palm trees narrowing the fairway 200 yards out. A bunker at front right guards the forward-sloping green. The fifth is a more pronounced dogleg right, pines and water lying on the inner angle. A deep front bunker guards the green.

The par-3 seventh measures 169 yards and carries over water. The green slopes to the front right quarter, where a bunker waits. Two par 4s finish the round. This nine supplies the best test of golf. If given the choice here in the northeast, play the South-West combination.

Bent Creek Golf Course

10440 Tournament Lane, Jacksonville 32222
(904) 779-0800
www.golfbentcreek.com

Green fee: $61

Architects: Bobby Weed and Mark McCumber, 1989
Par 71
Gold yardage 6,620; course rating 72.5; slope rating 131
Red yardage 5,021; course rating 69.4; slope rating 120

Directions: From I-295 exit 16, go west on 134 (103 Road Street) 4.4 miles. Entrance is on left.

From I-10 exit 351, go south on 115 (Chaffee Road) 4.4 miles. At 134 (103 Road Street) turn left. In 0.6 miles, entrance is on right.

The approach to the first.

For fifteen years the PGA Tour ran the Golf Club of Jacksonville. Times change, and in 2005 the Billy Casper Golf management group took control. The new head professional already had a handle on the place, having worked another course in the city. Bob Geppert knows his clientele—he knows that the people who'll be playing local PGA Tour courses won't be visiting Bent Creek. His angle is to cultivate repeat business and appeal to the local population. A busy evening crowd already uses the illuminated practice facilities that include a driving range, practice bunker, chipping areas, and putting greens. Now the team mission is to draw them back during daylight hours.

He calls Bent Creek a $25 course. Yes, the rack rate is more than twice that, but surprisingly the average round brings in $25. People have discount cards from health groups and golf associations, twilight fees affect the average, and those of us who pay annual dues are fully aware that the cost per round decreases the more we play. Geppert puts it more simply: "Not everybody plays on a weekend before midday." The annual funds needed to run and maintain a course are around $1 million. He says courses can get away with $750,000, but will be frayed at the edges; $1.25 million and happiness is guaranteed.

The mathematics are straightforward: 50,000 rounds per year @ $25 each = $1.25 million. Paying customers per day needed to accrue this amount = 137.

The eighteenth tee.

Assuming an average of eight hours available for starting times (less in winter, more in summer), this can be achieved by sending off two players every seven minutes. Groups of three and four balls are obviously more profitable or can allow longer intervals between tee times—eight minutes is more comfortable and ten minutes positively luxurious.

Bent Creek is a member of the Audubon Cooperative Sanctuary System, and preservation areas run throughout. Two-thirds of the holes have water as a lateral hazard. Trees form the other lining on fairways. The subdivision was never affiliated directly with the course, other than lending the new name, which regulars had used for years anyway. Trees, water, and housing make it a typical Florida course.

The 538-yard, par-5 first hole slides to the right between pine trees and chocolate-drop mounding. Bunkers lie at the 100-yard marker with one green-side and a rear pot. A 190-yard one-shot follows. The third doglegs right with a tee shot over wetland toward an aiming bunker at the 150-yard marker. Water runs 200 yards to the green on the right. Two saving bunkers sit greenside right, and the putting surface is almost flat, save for the tiniest hump at center left.

The 409-yard fourth fairway undulates wildly, with water again to the right. At the landing area it flattens and widens, with mounds covering the right-side approach. One tree and a bunker hem the left side of the green. Six, a par 5, forces a carry over wetland. A ribbon bunker to the left runs alongside the water, separating fairway from housing. Three pines and mounds are cross hazards to the right. The hole turns right at the end. Seven is a one-shot carry over wetland to a wide green with two rear pots and a front right bunker. The putting surface sheds to the extremities.

The eighth has water off the tee on both sides for the drive. A bunker sits left at the 150-yard marker. The angled green has a narrow entrance; a bunker at front left hides a small gully running between it and the green. Measuring 459 yards, eleven doglegs right, over wetlands with an inner-angle ribbon trap. More wetland must be crossed at the 150-yard marker. The green cornflakes from center right to front left quarter in the direction of a greenside bunker.

Twelve has a J-shaped tee with a water carry from the back tees. Forward tees have the water to the left. Grass hollows and mounds occupy the fairway's right side on the approach. The green is guarded by sand front and rear. Thirteen also is a hit over wetland to a wide landing area, curving left all the way for 395 yards. A pot bunker guards the front right, and grass hollows arc the green at the rear.

The fourteenth is a 220-yard one-shot with wetland to the left. The putting surface falls from front right to rear left. It was a daring move to build a house so close to the tee.

Fifteen, at 565 yards, is a three-shot hole and a par 5 with bite. Draw the tee shot around the corner and end up in a steep-faced, mounded bunker. The second-shot landing area has a large, shallow bunker on the left. The fairway narrows and carries over a gate of trees and wetland to the green.

Two par 4s finish the trip. On seventeen, a mounded bunker sits right at 200 yards, and the fairway widens beyond. Mounds and a stand of pines close off approach from the right. A crescent bunker sits to the right of the green. Eighteen is a fairly straight shot with bunkers on both sides after the 150-yard marker. Hollows surround the green.

Bob Geppert told me how he was with Billy Casper in California at a junior golf clinic. A young boy was flopping golf balls onto a green with a lob wedge. Casper interrupted him and demonstrated a few chips with a 6-iron, showing him there was more than one way of getting to the hole. The kid grunted and went back to his lobbing. According to Bob, children only want to learn two things nowadays: to smash the ball as far as they can with a driver, and to flop with a flipper.

Hyde Park Golf Club

6439 Hyde Grove Avenue, Jacksonville 32210
(904) 786-5410
www.hydeparkgolf.com

Green fee: $36

Architect: Donald Ross, 1925
Par 72 (blue), 73 (red)
Blue yardage 6,468; course rating 70.8; slope rating 122
Red yardage 5,464; course rating 71.3; slope rating 119

Directions: From I-295 exit 17, go east on 208 (Wilson Boulevard) 0.7 miles. At 103 (Lane Avenue) turn left. Go 1.0 miles to Hyde Grove Avenue and turn right. In 0.5 miles, entrance is on left.

From I-295 exit 19, go east on 228 (Normandy Boulevard) 1.2 miles. At 103 (Lane Avenue) turn right. Go 1.6 miles to Hyde Grove Avenue and turn left. In 0.5 miles, entrance is on left.

Watching the Players Championship at Sawgrass, some viewers may be unaware the tournament grew out of the Jacksonville Open, formerly held at Hyde Park. This club is saturated with history. All the greats in years gone by played at this venue. The Godfather of American Golf Architecture, Donald Ross, designed the track. Mickey Wright, winner of thirteen majors, scored her first LPGA victory here in 1956 and returned to win the next year.

Billy Maxwell and Chris Blocker, roommates on the PGA tour in the 1960s, have owned and run the place for more than thirty years. Billy Maxwell attended North Texas State and was U.S. Amateur Champion in 1951. He won eight tournaments after turning professional. Chris Blocker, an alumnus of Texas Tech, was also a winner on the professional tour, while cousin Dan sealed the fame of the family name with his character Hoss Cartwright in *Bonanza*.

The course plays fairly flat from the tees. There are gentle shifts in elevation, but not so much as to increase or impair roll. More variance in grade is noticeable on approaches, usually down into a creek then rising to the green. Tree-lined fairways are wide with few hazards. An old aerial photograph hanging in the clubhouse shows thirty missing bunkers. Legend has it that whenever the previous owner landed in one, he had it filled in. Pace of play was his justification.

On this Donald Ross course you don't come to drive, you come to hit into the greens and to putt. And boy, do you have to putt! The greens have hardly altered since 1925, and some defy logic, physics, mathematics, geometry, and trigonometry. On my first visit I borrowed an old putter and sampled the greens, which are admittedly kept on the fast side. Experimental long putts came up short time after time; when hit a bit harder, the ball sped off the green. Better to stay below the hole was the advice.

Number one starts easily at 372 yards with a wide fairway angling left. The raised, forward-pitching green has bunkers in front at both sides. The second, of similar length, has a tree barrier to the left off the tee and screams for a draw. A bunker lies 25 yards off the green to the left, and one sits greenside right. The green's surface is flatter than the first.

On three any drive of 240 yards or shorter will escape rolling into a water hazard crossing the fairway. This leaves an approach of around 150 yards. The fairway rises and narrows to the green, which slopes to front left. Bunkers guard both front quarters.

Hogan's Eleven.

A front pin placement suggests coming up short.

A photo of the 151-yard sixth on the scorecard almost gleefully declares, "This is the hole that brought him to his knees." Ben Hogan took an 11 here in the Jacksonville Open of 1947. A deep bunker pushes up the greenside front right, and water lies to the left. Hogan pulled a 7-iron into the water. After twice trying unsuccessfully to get out, he opted for a lift and drop. He flubbed into the water, took another lift and drop, then chipped on and two-putted. I took a seven here with a putter off the tee. My achievement was small and hollow, Hogan's merely noble folly. The greenside water hazard had no bulkhead in 1947 as it does now.

Nine has a shallow cross bunker 255 yards from the tee. Two long bunkers run from 75 yards to 25 yards off the raised green. The putting surface slopes forward, with bunkers at both sides.

The back nine begins with a par 5 curling right. The raised green has mounds at every corner, making three-putts a sure bet. Eleven is a 185-yard par 3 over a water hazard with a bunker to the right. The putting surface pitches forward, and a front pin placement suggests coming up short to be below the hole.

Twelve's green has a bowl in the right center. Mounds before and behind it turn this cupping area into bogey territory. The 347-yard thirteenth plays uphill, with a fairway bunker 125 yards from the elevated teardrop green. The front flows forward and is guarded on both sides by sand hazards. Fourteen plays to a broad and level landing area. From 200 yards it slides left, down and over a creek, then uphill to a green with a gentle break and a bunker at the right side.

The finishing holes are classic Ross. Fifteen's 409 yards play over a water hazard and up to an accentuated crown green. Hitting into this target, if you're short, the ball sticks; if left, it bounces away to the rough; if right, it spills into a greenside pot. Sixteen is a picturesque par 3 of 178 yards guarded only by a bunker at front left.

The seventeenth drops from a slightly elevated tee and goes left, where it is flanked by a ditch and a tree barrier. Aim for the landing area to the right. The raised green is winged by bunkers at the front and gathers forward to a central funnel. The home hole fades off the tee. Humps and swales take over the right side on the approach. Two left-side bunkers guard the green, the course's largest at more than 10,000 square feet. The putting surface slopes to the right.

Hyde Park's greens are rounds or ovals and average 6,000 square feet, but vary greatly in size from hole to hole. Nine and sixteen are less than 4,500 square feet. The par 3s, six and eleven, are around 5,000, while four and seven are in the 6,000-square-foot range. One and five measure closer to 7,000 square feet. Approach, variety of green size, and slope are keys to the green complexes that will have the purist returning to Hyde Park, tucked away in this leafy suburb of old Jacksonville.

Windsor Parke Golf Club

13823 Sutton Park Drive, Jacksonville 32224
(904) 223-4653
www.windsorparke.com

Green fee: $60 (doubles during TPC week at Sawgrass)

Architect: Arthur Hills, 1989
Par 72
Blue yardage 6,435; course rating 71.1; slope rating 132
Red yardage 5,206; course rating 71.5; slope rating 125

*Directions: From I-95 exit 344, go east on 202 (Butler Boulevard) 7.4 miles
and take Hodges Boulevard exit. In 0.3 miles, at Hodges Boulevard, turn left.
Go 0.4 miles to Sutton Park Drive and turn right. Entrance is in 0.7 miles,
on right.*

Windsor Parke lies at the heart of Jacksonville's new urban landscape midway
between Jacksonville Beach and the eastern ring of what will someday become
the city's peripheral Interstate 295. The old city lies west of the St. Johns River
and to the north where the river narrows abruptly and changes course a time
or two, as if shaking free from the land.

Modern development along Butler Boulevard seems as fresh as newly
minted coin, but the golf course has been here for more than fifteen years.
Windsor Parke loops clockwise past an elementary school and the eye-catching
offices of a trucking logistics company; the building's modern International
style is the very essence of today's business park communal workspace envi-
ronment. The front nine continues past a hotel, a small mall, and condos built
behind the water barriers on eight and nine. The back nine's neighbors are
purely residential. The middle holes go around the block in the most pleasing
five-hole stretch at this track. The other four form a green corridor 900 yards
long.

Tee boxes at number one point into the trees on the right. The hole drifts
that way after the 150-yard marker, and two trees cover the right approach. The
angled green has a hump at center left and sheds predominantly back right. The

An-all-the-way-around-a-lake-to-the-left hole.

second is a 155-yard one-shot to an elevated green. Propped up on the right side, the surface cants to the left. A trio of bunkers guards the front gate.

Three is a par 5 with generous landing area for the drive and a pot bunker to the left, 200 yards from green center. The left tree line partially masks the green, and getting home in two will need a draw. A shallow bunker sits right at 100 yards. The second landing area leaves a chip over two front bunkers to the target.

The fifth tee shot plays to a shelf, 175 to 150 yards from the green. Five bunkers occupy mounds to the left, and the fairway tilts right toward water, which covers the approach. One front bunker guards the green; a bailout area lies to the left.

Water is a feature on every hole for the remainder of this half. On the sixth it separates the right from the landmark office building. Golfing workers play a scramble on Monday afternoons. The fairway runs out at 100 yards, leaving only mounded rough or a punt over water. Bunkers lie at the front and rear left.

The seventh is rated hardest hole; a 170-yard tee shot is needed to reach the fairway. Water cuts diagonally in front of the tee and runs the length of play to the left. Eight similarly has water as a left-side barrier; a berm mound defines the other side of this par 5. The fairway is wide and fairly flat for a hundred yards until the 150-yard marker. Two bunkers flank the green entrance, and one waits at rear left.

The ninth curls to the right, again with water on the left and a ribbon stand of trees at the midsection. A waste area planted with cordgrass covers the approach, and the green tilts toward the water. Twelve is a 130-yard par 3 with its target squeezed between tall mounds planted with pines. The putting surface is like a saddle. The tee faces the front right quarter.

Thirteen skirts a lake to the left for 388 yards. This brand of hole can be seen at LPGA International's Legends Course and at Cypress Head, all by Arthur Hills with Mike Dasher assisting. Bunkers are placed to the right at 175 yards and 125 yards with one greenside. In my scribbled notes this has become the "all-the-way-left-around-a-lake hole."

Another Hills trait is the single tree within a hundred yards of the green, hindering aerial approach to one half of the target. Fourteen is a 307-yard par 4. A long bunker with a tree at the far end inhibits aim from the right. Three shallow and circular bunkers guard the elevated green.

Fifteen, a 533-yard par 5, allows a wide landing area between pine trees. A shelf runs to the right until 222 yards from green center; the fairway drops, then narrows at the 150-yard marker. Water cuts across the green front, so a layup to wedge distance is the safe play for all but the longest hitters. Sixteen plays 182 yards over water to a peninsula green (see color plate 2). A thin, crescent bunker rings the target from left to rear; two conventional hazards sit to the mounded side.

If you feel as though you're being watched on the seventeenth tee, the surrounding woods are home to a family of foxes. The fairway narrows into a gully on approach, and bunkers circle the small green. At the last, water runs all the way right and forces a wee carry from the back tees. The fairway tilts toward the drink, and the green angles to the right. A sand hazard at front left and a bailout area behind provide a better option than flirting with water again.

Windsor Parke is pretty and user friendly. Water, a lateral hazard to separate play from buildings, forces only a couple of tough carries. Holes play mostly straight, with some sliders and greens tucked away. The fairways are not over-bunkered, although both five and thirteen have large clusters. Most of the forty sand hazards are greenside. Putting surfaces measure around 4,000 square feet, enough to allow a modicum of undulation. Windsor Parke betrays false modesty by regularly hosting U.S. Amateur and Public Links Qualifiers.

9

Meadowbrook Golf Club

3200 NW 98th Street, Gainesville 32606
(352) 332-0577
www.gainesvillesbestgolf.com

Green fee: $36

Architect: Steve Smyers, 1987
Par 72
Blue yardage 6,276; course rating 71.5; slope rating 126
Red yardage 4,519; course rating 67.5; slope rating 114

*Directions: From I-75 exit 390, go west on 222 (NW 39th Avenue) 0.3 miles.
At NW 98th Street turn left. Entrance is on right in 0.5 miles.*

A quirky course routed through woodland hill and dale with six par 3s, six par 4s, and six par 5s. Both sides have three par 5s; the front plays 750 yards shorter and two strokes lower, having four of the par 3s. Elevation changes on every hole. Half the holes elbow or dogleg. Some have bunkers, others none. Water factors on six occasions, and greens average 5,000 square feet but vary considerably in size and shape. Five alternate tee placements shorten length from the blues by 270 yards. Four single-hole corridors connect three parcels of land where groups of holes are laid out in a tight core pattern.

This is an early solo design of Steve Smyers, himself a graduate of the University of Florida in Gainesville and member of the winning Gators 1973 NCAA golf team. Compared to Southern Dunes in Haines City (see chapter 28), Meadowbrook is an interesting harbinger of his later, more expansive style, particularly in bunkering.

The first hole offers a birdie, thank you very much, for a par 5 of only 417 yards. A downhill fade avoids two collection bunkers covering the outer angle 175 to 125 yards from the green. The fairway tilts left on approach, and mounding covers the right all the way to greenside, with runoff to the left. Two is a scenic 167-yard par 3 through a chute of trees and over water (see color plate 3). The green, guarded by a pot bunker at front right, slopes forward and to the left.

At the 451-yard third, the approach narrows significantly from the 150-yard marker, with tall pines lining each side. The green feeds to the front right, and a bunker drapes from the left for 25 yards. Five's blind tee shot plays over a V-shaped gully; the hole is appropriately named the Chute. The landing area rises to a shelf 150 to 100 yards from the target. A downhill approach to a narrow green, angling right, must clear a pot bunker at the front left corner.

Six needs a 186-yard drive to carry a pond, which also features on the par-3 seventh. The fairway elbows right and uphill another 122 yards to the target, guarded at the rear. Seven has two options for length from the blue tees: 218 or 188 yards. The shot is downhill, over the pond to a rising green table. The putting surface pours forward from a hump at center left, and a bunker sits below the right side.

The eighth is only 142 yards, running uphill alongside the seventh. This pair of back-to-back par 3s is followed by back-to-back par 5s. Nine runs uphill through a narrow, tree-lined fairway with a ribbon bunker to the right at driving distance. At 478 yards, it is chancy to go for the green in two, as a brace of deep bunkers waits greenside right. A generous bailout area lies wide of these hazards. A similar predicament faces the three-shot play, as three flashed cross bunkers occupy the fairway 90 yards from the flag.

Beginnings of monumental bunkering.

Number ten, Big Easy, is a mere five yards longer than nine, but it plays downhill from the 200-yard marker. The green, more than 40 yards deep and 10 yards wide, slopes left. Trees line the left-hand side of eleven, encroaching on the greenside. The green complex is raised, and three pots guard the front at this 160-yard one-shot.

The next three play alternately up and down a hillside at the highest point of the course. Water lies at the base, affecting the tee shots on twelve and fourteen and the approach to the thirteenth green. Twelve's tee shot must carry 150 yards to reach the fairway, which curls uphill to the left. The kidney-shaped green slopes to front left.

Thirteen's water cuts into the fairway at the 200-yard marker. Serving as aiming markers for the second shot at this par 5, two pot bunkers lie pin-high 70 yards from the green. Fourteen requires another long carry off the tee. Although an alternative blue tee reduces by 50 yards the 430-yard length, Dead-man's Curve is rated hardest hole. The fairway tilts left on the uphill approach. The bell-shaped green is unguarded and steps down from the rear portion to the front right quarter.

Fifteen has a similarly shaped undulating green. Three deep bunkers front the target at this 162-yard downhill one-shot. Sixteen heads into the Canyon, then curves and climbs to an unprotected plateau green tucked away to the left.

Seventeen continues uphill to a shelf at the right side of the fairway. A lower path to the left runs toward a gully and creek that cross diagonally to the right and cut off the green. The putting surface slopes forward, and the architect displays a fair attitude in deciding the gully and creek afford the target enough protection.

Eighteen, called the Valley, tumbles downhill from the tee and kicks right at the first landing area on this 595- or 545-yarder. The left side gives better placement for a second shot. Gently ascending from the 150-yard marker, the fairway rises more steeply from 75 yards out. Staggered pot bunkers cover the approach to a deep and narrow green. The putting surface cascades in three defined steps from rear right to center left, and to front right.

In Lakeland, just north of I-4 exit 33, exists a community golf course called the Sandpiper, a Steve Smyers design contemporary with Meadowbrook. If you intend to tackle Southern Dunes, it is worth your while to experience this architect's early traits and flourishes.

10

Ironwood Golf Course

2100 NE 39th Avenue, Gainesville 32609
(352) 334-3120
www.ironwoodgolf.net

Green fee: $31

Architect: David Wallace, 1963
Par 72
Blue yardage 6,465; course rating 71.3; slope rating 126
Red yardage 5,259; course rating 70.7; slope rating 119

*Directions: From I-75 exit 390, take 222 (39th Avenue) east for 9.0 miles;
entrance is on left.*

*From 24 (Waldo Road) junction with 222 (39th Avenue), go west on 222 for
0.5 miles; entrance is on right.*

An old house after renovation, or furniture improving with age—that's Ironwood. Built by an independent developer as a nine-hole course in 1964, it had
its back nine added three years later. As many struggling golf course owners
have discovered, it's no quick buck, this relationship with the land; like a farm,
it needs attention on a daily basis. Every superintendent will testify that he can
lavish care on his course for fifty weeks of the year and return after a two-week
vacation to find a goat ranch. One superintendent said a long weekend is all
he can manage without going crazy thinking about what's happening to his
greens.

Ironwood in the 1980s was less than affectionately known as Ironweed.
Turnaround began when the city of Gainesville bought the property in 1992
for $1.2 million and made the astute move of hiring Bill Iwinski as head profes-
sional and manager. How could they possibly lose with a name like that!

The front side loops out to the north for three holes, fiddles around for
three, and returns to the clubhouse. The back nine heads northwest for five
holes and comes home in four. The single fairways pull the player inexorably
on, a progression reminiscent of Pinehurst. Tree barriers lining every hole are,
well, pines. Water plays more of a role on the front nine than on the back,

That Pinehurst appearance.

with no drastically penal carries. Bunkers are conventional shapes, the majority placed greenside. Greens are round and average 4,800 square feet; the front nine average more than 5,000, the back closer to 4,300 square feet.

A par 5 of 500 yards kicks off the round, with a no-worry pond fronting the tee. A bunker lies left at the 250-yard marker. Water sits right from 160 yards and becomes a creek crossing the fairway 60 yards before the green. A bailout area lies over the creek to the left. The green slopes away from front right; two bunkers guard that quarter.

On two the creek runs diagonally from the right across the driving line; 160 yards clears it, and the water becomes a lateral hazard with 180 yards remaining. The target is tucked away to the right with a front left bunker. The putting surface feeds to the center and then forward.

The third is rated hardest hole, a 420-yard par 4. From a narrow chute with a thick tree barrier to the right and singles on the left, the tee shot plays to a generous landing area. Water begins left at 180 yards and widens into a cross hazard between the 150- and 100-yard markers. Three lone pines to the right squeeze this section of the approach, which is safe from there on. The green's left side is guarded by hazards front and rear.

A bunker guarding the right corner is the only defense at the 173-yard fourth. The featherweight green measures 3,420 square feet. On five, trees border the right; a few break rank like spectators peeking out to look back down the fairway. Left of center is best placement for the drive; bunkers sit front right and side left. The small, coin-shaped green tilts forward.

Six is a one-shot of 210 yards. How refreshing to have a par 3 with a single-digit stroke index, 7 in this case. The target sheds from the rear left quarter and is fairly flat in the opposing corner. A bunker catches anything immediately short and left.

Seven by contrast is a medium-length par 4 and easiest hole on this side. Water lines the first 200 yards to the left, and a sparse stand of tall pines cuts into the right-hand side of the landing area. The fairway widens on approach to an elevated green with a bunker covering the front left quarter. Humps at the edges of the putting surface push balls into the center, and toward the greenside hazard.

Ten might be rated easiest hole, but two tall pines stand halfway along the 141 yards of this one-shot. The green has a marked horizontal channel at center left. Eleven curves right from a narrow chute of pines. Right of center is the best approach, since a front left bunker guards the cornflake green.

Twelve is a par 5, again with a narrow chute for the drive. Tree stands stagger the second landing area at 175 yards and a sand hazard lies to the right 50 yards beyond. A bunker drapes from left of the small green. Thirteen's thin fairway slides right. Pines take the place of a bunker greenside left, although sand guards the opposite side (see color plate 4). Fourteen plays 157 yards over water and a sand hazard at front left. The putting surface has humps at rear left and right center.

The four closing holes provide a friendly finish: three par 4s under 400 yards and the 504-yard seventeenth. Fifteen doglegs right and favors a tee shot left of center. A bunker sits greenside right with plenty of safety to the left and behind. Conversely, sixteen doglegs left. Water lies to the right of the landing area. The approach is open save for a greenside bunker at the front left quarter.

Seventeen angles left and, rather than sand, trees placed at the 150-yard marker make second-shot placement the important play. The green has a vertical spine in the front half, shedding left and right, but gathers to the center at the rear. The last hole has water to the right from the tee and shapes left on the approach. Bunkers sit 60 yards off the green and at greenside.

The course is now making money for the city. The rates are as much as a college-town municipal can charge without alienating the student population. Ironwood's green fee is a considerable bargain for both town and gown.

11

- - - - - - - - - - - -

Ocala Golf Club

3130 East Silver Springs Boulevard, Ocala 34470
(352) 401-6917

Green fee: $30

Architect: William F. Gordon, 1947
Par 72
Blue yardage 6,381; course rating 70.0; slope rating 119
Red yardage 5,106; course rating 69.8; slope rating 120

*Directions: From I-75 exit 352, take 40 east for 5.7 miles; entrance is on
the right.*

Despite a healthy dispute over the identity of the architect, Ocala Golf Club has a rich history. The original nine-hole course was an accompaniment to the old Highlands Hotel and designed by John Duncan Dunn around 1900, while he was in charge of building courses for the Florida West Coast Railroad. The clubhouse and hotel were beside today's seventh tee, where condominiums now stand. The seventh was the old first; today's sixth was the finishing hole. The Birmingham Barons, a farm team of the Boston Red Sox, lodged at the hotel, and Ted Williams frequented the course during spring training. In the 1940s, the city purchased the course for the measly sum of $15,000—perhaps the best club ever found in golf's bargain basement! The city wanted a new clubhouse and entrance on Silver Springs Boulevard, so in 1947 the front nine routing was changed and the back nine added.

For walkers, this is a cardiac course of four seriously uphill holes and four others downhill. Fairways are lined with trees, thin pines in the majority accompanied by oaks and some palms. Only three carries are over water. Two doglegs on the back nine add spice to what is otherwise a straight track. Of thirty bunkers, all but two are greenside; the exceptions, on seven and seventeen, are at landing areas.

William F. Gordon receives credit in Geoffrey Cornish and Ron Whitten's *The Architects of Golf* for the full design of Ocala Municipal No. 1, as it was known. Gordon worked for golf architects Toomey and Flynn for eighteen

The old first, now the seventh.

years. Although he started his own business in 1941, he did war duty in seeding work for military installations. After the war he built courses for Donald Ross and J. B. McGovern and also began designing independently.

A charter member of the American Society of Golf Course Architects, he appears in the celebrated photograph of that illustrious gathering at Pinehurst in 1948. In 1946 he designed nine holes at Fairfax Country Club in Virginia, and the next year he undertook Ocala. To quote Cornish and Whitten, "Probably no other architect in history received such broad practical experience before setting up his own practice, nor was any more imbued with the history of the art."

The six-hundred-year-old oak.

David W. Gordon, William's son, must be acknowledged for his input; he is a past president of the American Society of Golf Course Architects. Lloyd Clifton, Ken Ezell, and George Clifton similarly deserve recognition for renovating all of Ocala's greens and tees in 1989.

The first is wide open and tree-lined. Pines ring the rear of the green, which has conventional front bunkers. Two is a penal par 3, 154 yards over water. The green has a gentle forward slope and two rear bunkers. The third hikes 368 yards uphill to a plateau green with two bunkers to the right. Trees lining the fairway are shared barriers with holes on either side.

Four tumbles downhill toward the lake fronting the second green. The ground rises sharply to the front-bunkered target. A vertical ridge at the rear sheds left and right. Next, a par 5 of 503 yards runs to the high ground once more. The fairway tilts to the left and narrows at the 100-yard marker; a stand of pines blocks approach from the right. The plateau green is tucked away to the right with a front left bunker and a punchbowl surface.

The seventh plays 487 yards downhill to a raised green with a drop-off behind. Bunkers pinch the entrance at both sides. The following par 3 echoes this green configuration.

A plaque by the clubhouse commemorates Jim Yancey, the pro here for twenty-six years from 1970. The inscription reads: "His life was spent as a champion on the athletic field and in our community . . . promoting golf and supporting the youth of Marion County and Florida." His brother Bert was a Tour player who came close to winning the Masters in 1967.

Bert Yancey was so obsessed by the Masters that he knew who made Augusta National's flagsticks. It is said he had models of the greens built as aide-mémoire in preparation. Depressed by his failure, he contemplated missing the next tournament, in those days the Dallas Open. Showing regal compassion, Arnold Palmer persuaded him to compete. He told him he was playing well and should keep on the roll. The King flew him to Dallas in his private plane. Over Augusta National, Arnie lifted the plane into a vertical climb as if to tell Yancey to leave his loss behind. Yancey dropped his cookies on the plane ride, but he won the Dallas Open the next week.

The Yancey family runs the Henry Camp Memorial Tournament at Ocala every April. This hotly contested amateur event is one of the oldest aside from the Florida State Amateur and predates Ocala's reputation as horse country.

Ten's fairway rises and slopes left. The first green with any significant undulation, it gathers to cupping areas at front left and center right. Twelve romps downhill angling slightly to the right. Bunkers sit behind and front left of the green, which falls from rear left. The par-5 thirteenth doglegs left 492 yards. The ground rises from the 150-yard marker, and one front bunker protects the target.

Sixteen slogs uphill to a green with a false front but no hazards. Seventeen has a fairway bunker at the first landing area. The green has two wing bunkers at the front. The home hole kicks right with 140 yards remaining. Two deep pot bunkers guard the front of the elevated green.

A noteworthy oak stands regally between the seventeenth green and eighteenth tee. Estimated to be more than six hundred years old, it was already a centenarian when Mary Queen of Scots played golf the day after her second husband died. How golf soothes the grieving soul.

LPGA *International*

1000 Champions Drive, Daytona Beach 32124
(386) 274-5742
www.lpgainternational.com

Green fee: $100–$140 for two courses

Champions		Legends
Rees Jones, 1994	Architect	Arthur Hills, 1998
72	Par	72
6,225	Yardage (white tees)	6,339
77.3/145	Course/Slope ratings (women)	77.3/144
70.3/124	Course/Slope ratings (men)	70.9/132

Directions: From I-95 exit 265, go west on LPGA Boulevard 0.5 miles. Turn left into LPGA International property (Champions Drive); entrance is in 2.4 miles on right.

The miserable faces I saw on golf courses in Florida all belonged to men. Every lady I met, without exception, gave a smile and a cheery greeting. However stark the gender contrast, the white tees at both LPGA courses are compatible with handicaps ranging from 9 to 19 for men and from scratch to 4 for ladies. Hackers (who have come to terms with their own inadequacies) would all benefit from moving farther forward to the gold tees to ensure smiles all round.

Arthur Hills's Legends Course is shaped like the figure 9. The front side forms the loop running counterclockwise. The back nine is a straight two-hole corridor, the sequence weaving from side to side. Hazards include fifty bunkers: grass faced, rounded shapes in the main. Water is a lateral feature on half a dozen holes; wetland scrub forces a carry more often. Dense stands of thin pines are the dominant furniture on Legends, particularly on the back nine, making the impression of tight courts with vertical boundaries.

As payback for a 362-yard loosener, the par-5 second is rated most difficult hole on this side; for ladies, the eighth has this distinction. A carry of 150 yards over wetland sets up a dogleg left. A ribbon trap runs the length of the left side, the green tucked away. Four, a short par 4, kicks right, and requires a carry over wetland on approach. A bunker guards the left side.

Six and eight both curl around a lake to the left in trademark Hills fashion. Six, a par 4 of 382 yards, has the more defined angle and a large bunker at greenside right. Eight, a 509-yard par 5, is more of a slider. Two bunkers sit in the center of the wide fairway at 199 and 273 yards from the tee respectively. A higher shelf of fairway lies to the right. The play narrows considerably from 85 yards in. Three pots and a couple of grass hollows play roulette with the approach. The thinnest of collars saves the lake from lapping onto the green.

The back nine really puts on the pressure from the fourteenth—rated hardest hole for ladies—a 502-yard elbow to the right. Carried over wetland, the tee shot faces two shallow bunkers with rear mounds covering the right side at 175 and 275 yards. Beyond, directly in line with these, is a center fairway bunker. The green is tucked away, elevated and guarded in front by two sand hazards. A bailout area allows missing the green to the left.

After a breather at the one-shot fifteenth, sixteen weighs in at 510 yards with water running the entire length to the right. To the left, a bunker 225 yards off the tee and surrounding banking leaves a second shot over a pot bunker at

Grass-faced, polite bunkering.

the 150-yard marker. The green slopes to the water, and a bunker waits at rear left.

Eighteen is rated Legends' hardest hole for men. On this dogleg left, 230 yards are needed to pass a large oak at the corner. Facing yet another approach over wetland, it struck me that on this course the play's the thing and putting is a secondary pleasure.

Rees Jones's Champions Course is short-grain rice compared to long-grain Legends. It feels more open, bald if you like, and its perimeter complexion has changed with the addition of more housing. Water is in play on half the holes, and as a forced carry off the tee on one, two, thirteen, and a couple of the par 3s, six and seventeen. Bunkers number around eighty, with pots large and small, and amorphous shapes for large collection bunkers without "capes"—tongues of grass protruding into the sand. Bunkers on thirteen and fourteen have bullets, or islands of grass, within them (see color plate 5); nine's midsection is riddled with pots on either side. A number of sand hazards measure 50 yards or longer, and bunkers guard every green, bar the final pair, on at least two sides. Greens are traditional round and oval shapes; tiers, humps, and hollows give them internal variety.

A tee shot over water, which curves to the left, begins. A large collection bunker sits to the right, 194 yards from the tee. A similar water clearance of 130 yards is needed at the second. A drive of 202 yards will pass the large fairway bunker, placed to the left this time. A bunker drapes from the left side of the green, the right side guarded by a smaller hazard. The green is round and pitches forward from a rear left shelf.

The fifth is a 469-yard par 5 with water all the way right. Six is a penal one-shot of 137 yards over water. A front bunker guards the green and a larger one sits to the left. The putting surface sheds from an elevated segment rear right.

The ninth fairway is a chute lined by mounds for most of its 522 yards. A smattering of pot bunkers stretches for 90 yards around the second landing area. The round green has one large bunker to the left and a pot at rear right. The 356-yard eleventh demands a draw from the tee to avoid 80 yards of bunkering at the landing area. Bunkers surrounding the green make aerial approach a requirement. The green slopes to the front right quarter from a small tier at rear left.

The thirteenth is a spectacular 533-yard par 5 and rated hardest hole for both sexes. Mounds and hollows run the entire left side; all the trouble lies to the right. A drive of 175 yards should clear an intimidating lake; beyond sits an 80-yard-long bunker with two grass bullets. A similar hazard lies at the second landing area, also with water to the right. Bunkers guard the heavily mounded green at front right and greenside left.

The 148-yard seventeenth tries to steal the limelight; it plays over water to a peninsula green with a single bunker at front right.

LPGA International has extensive practice facilities with putting and chipping greens, a 360-yard double-ended driving range, and three practice holes. The property is home to the Ladies Professional Golf Association headquarters, hence the name. However, the association has no involvement in the day-to-day running of the facility. Nevertheless, the venue proves the perfect fit for the final rounds of LPGA Qualifying School and an excellent showcase for the women's game.

13

Daytona Beach Golf Club—
North Course

600 Wilder Boulevard, Daytona Beach 32114
(386) 671-3500
www.ci.daytona-beach.fl.us/golfcourse

Green fee: $40

Architect: Slim Deathridge, 1946
Par 72
Blue yardage 6,338; course rating 71.8; slope rating 137
Red yardage 4,971; course rating 69.1; slope rating 117

Directions: From I-95 exit 260A, take 400 (Beville Road) east 4.6 miles to US 1
(Ridgewood Avenue). Turn left (north) and go 0.4 miles. At Wilder Boulevard
turn left; entrance is in 0.3 miles.

Railway tracks run through the eastern side of Daytona Beach Golf Club, a reminder of how the sport was first brought here. The symbiosis of trains, winter
resorts, and golf is an integral part of Florida's development during the nineteenth and twentieth centuries. Automobile racing supersedes all at Daytona
Beach, but for those who prefer sport at a slower pace, the municipal facility
has thirty-six holes to offer.

It's unusual to pass over a Donald Ross design in favor of a virtual unknown;
at Daytona Beach I think it is a worthy choice. The Godfather of American
Golf Architecture had laid out the South Course in 1921. Today one can still
sample its parallel holes, forgiving landing areas, testing approach shots, and
large greenside hazards.

A quarter century later the head professional saw a need for expansion at
the club. Slim Deathridge (great name!) certainly knew his Ross and built the
North Course in a similar fashion. Slim chanced his arm and went all out to
outdo. In my view he succeeded. During a makeover in 1997 by Lloyd Clifton,
Ken Ezell, and George Clifton all tees, bunkers, and greens were renovated.

Like a four-toed paw print.

The North Course is shaped like the letter *p*, while the South is a letter *d*; the two nestle close like a yin-and-yang symbol. North's front nine occupies the vertical bar, a corridor with a thick tree barrier. Pines, palms, and oaks shrink the fairways with mature overhang. The back nine fills in the bulbous loop—a core routing, yet these holes have a more open feel. Water forces a carry on three of the par 3s, and only four holes are completely dry. Bunkers are on the massive side of large; any larger and they'd be grotesque.

Number one measures 338 yards. The fairway angles left in the final third, with water to the right. As an indication of what to expect, a voluminous two-bay bunker props up the greenside front left.

Four is a 526-yard par 5 and rated hardest hole on the course. A dalliance with water off the tee will harm only feeble chunks and hits from the hosel. A shallow bunker lies to the right around the 250-yard marker. Two more bunkers gouge deep into the right side of the raised green, also guarded at the rear. The putting surface flows to the left and forward from the rear right quarter.

The fifth doglegs left 316 yards with water covering the inner angle. King-size sand hazards front the crown green. On six, a one-shot of 152 yards over water,

View along thirteen.

the green slopes to the right. A monster cape bunker impresses the greenside front like a four-toed paw print.

Number eight, a par 5 of 485 yards, elbows left at the turning point. A bunker sits 50 yards off the green to the right; a pond sits greenside left. Two deep bunkers collect anything overshooting the flattish putting surface. The ninth doglegs right, the fairway merely 16 yards wide at the 100-yard marker. Two front sand hazards narrow the green entrance to 11 yards.

On the tenth, a decent drive should clear the (I fumble for superlatives) immense bunker located to the left. Water at the 170-yard eleventh is not long, but a distraction nonetheless. A sand hazard sits to the right of the target. Twelve's tee shot demands a full 170 yards of clearance; water lies to the right and in front on the drive. The raised green, 318 yards distant, is guarded on the left side.

Thirteen runs a straight 378 yards. An eccentrically shaped cape bunker eats into the front right quarter of the crown green. The fourteenth tee box stands at the northwestern extremity of the course. The 163-yard one-shot plays to a raised green complex with sand guarding both sides.

Fifteen doglegs to the right at the 150-yard marker with water on the outer angle. The tabletop green is unguarded and slopes forward. The next, a short par 4, has a small water carry off the tee and two bunkers right of the landing area. Another bunker sits left, 50 yards off the green, which is triangled by oval pots.

The last two are back-to-back par 5s and rated most difficult holes on this half.

Seventeen's slender fairway turns leftward. Water cuts directly in front of the green, and two sand hazards wait behind. The home hole needs 125 yards to reach dry land with 398 yards to go. Stands of pine trees and then a lake take over the right-hand side. The elevated green has cape bunkers at front left and rear right; the putting surface sheds from a central ridge.

Crossing back over the railroad tracks, I moved a few blocks away to the Museum of Arts and Sciences, off Route 5's Nova Road, where two train carriages from the 1950s are on display in the Root Family galleries. The Roots traveled between Chicago and Florida in these cars.

Chapman Jay Root founded the Root Glass Company in Terre Haute, Indiana, in 1901. One of his employees, Alexander Samuelson, is named in U.S. Patent 48160, issued November 16, 1915, as designer of the hobble skirt Coca-Cola bottle, inspired by an illustration of a cocoa bean pod. Mr. Root wintered in Florida yachting and golfing. His grandson Chapman Show Root moved the Root Glass Company to Daytona in 1951, and it then became the largest independent bottler of the successful soda. Grandson Root sponsors an automobile racing team. In his grandfather's day, cars raced along Daytona's beach. The speedway is four miles inland now, much noisier than a museum, and a little bit noisier than a golf course at times.

14

- - - - - - - - - - - -

The Golf Club at Cypress Head

6231 Palm Vista Street, Port Orange 32128
(386) 756-5449
www.cypressheadgolf.com

Green fee: $58

Architect: Arthur Hills, 1992
Par 72
Blue yardage 6,362; course rating 70.8; slope rating 130
Red yardage 4,909; course rating 69.3; slope rating 123

Directions: From I-95 exit 256, take 421 (Taylor Road) west 0.1 miles. At Williamson Boulevard turn left and go 2.2 miles. Bear right at Airport Road. In 0.2 miles, at Cypress Springs Parkway, turn left and go 0.7 miles to Palm Vista Street. Turn left; entrance is ahead.

Cypress Head is arranged in corridors of single holes. A clockwise loop goes out to the west containing back-to-back par 3s. The back nine trails counterclockwise in a longer string eastward, finishing with two par 5s. Houses are set back beyond water barriers. Water features mainly as a lateral hazard and forces carries over wetland off tees and on approaches. Incorporating only forty bunkers gives a kindly aspect to this public course. Greens are generous in size and undulate accordingly. Birdlife exists in abundance, and rabbits hop about the undergrowth.

After a 332-yard warm-up, the 507-yard second doglegs right and is rated hardest hole. Trees and wetland at the inner angle cut into the fairway 200 yards from the green. The next section of fairway, 150–100 yards, gives opportunity for a layup and a third shot. A small stand of cypress trees narrows the approach to the right and masks the useful greenside mounding; a thicket of trees borders the left edge of a strip of wetland fronting the green. The putting surface spills toward a greenside bunker at front left and falls away at the rear.

A wide landing area welcomes tee shots of many shapes at the 383-yard third. From the 150-yard marker a lake juts in front of the green. A wood stork thrusts its beak intently into the water, as if searching for a lost contact lens. The green sheds forward from two humps in the putting surface.

Water forces a carry from the tee at the 365-yard fourth. A lake curls into the fairway right of the landing area; the hole then kicks right over a small creek. A lone pine covers the right approach. The wide green slopes left and right from a central hump. Here a tricolored heron and snowy egret distract me with their antics: a peculiar dance of running, flapping at each other, flying and landing in synch, finally wading together and alternately ducking heads in the water. I realize theirs is a nagging friendship.

Six and seven are back-to-back par 3s. The sixth plays 185 yards over wetlands through a chute of trees; a ribbon bunker drapes forward from the left side of the green. The next is 40 yards shorter, with a pair of shallow dot bunkers at the front, the green wide this time instead of deep. Sparrows chase and worry a redwing blackbird in the halting turns and twisting darts of avian acrobatics.

Eight is the water hole on this half, a par 5 of 510 yards. There's a wide landing area for the tee shot, with a ribbon bunker to the right the only hazard. The lake comes into play for the last 200 yards; to the right a thin arc of fairway

A loaded approach and green complex at two.

A long carry on thirteen.

bows around to the green. A third shot still requires a water carry to reach the target, which is guarded by mounds to the right, a C-shaped bunker in front, and two little shallow ones behind. A mother moorhen dabs the water. Two tiny chicks mimic her bobbing, but their beaks look too small to hold even the smallest morsel.

Ten's green is settled in a hollow surrounded by mounds and ringed by trees. A little gully skirts the green to the left. As I head for the next tee, a red-tailed hawk flies over my shoulder and perches in an oak, his gaze questioning: "Come on, come on, where was that rabbit you said you saw?"

Thirteen requires a long carry for the high handicapper, 180 yards to reach dry land. A split blue tee allows this to be played as a 315-yard par 4, shorter by nearly 50 yards.

Fourteen is a big hole, a ninety-degree dogleg left around a lake, a 446-yard crescent really. Aiming bunkers indicate safe play for the majority of players. From the first landing zone the fairway bumbles along, constricting ever as the water intrudes. A lone bunker provides a bit of width between green and water hazard.

In the bushes behind the fourteenth, a straddling cardinal cocks his eye at me with a brown tentacle dangling from his beak. For the first time in my life I am close enough to say out loud: "No thanks, cardinal, I don't want your worm in my mouth."

Fifteen curls right, offering a broad landing area as the architect's reward for a decent drive. A lake to the left borders the approach, cutting in front of the target. A bunker at front right squeezes the entrance to the two-tiered green; the front half pitches forward. Under the trees to the right, two doves scratch around together, courting perhaps, or a young couple shopping around for nest-building material.

At sixteen, a slightly uphill par 3 with a very undulating green surrounded by bunkers, a blue heron paces about the tee. Like a gowned lawyer, hands behind his back, striding around a courthouse corridor, he waits with an annoyed glare for those four seniors to putt out.

Two par 5s finish this golfing ornithology. Seventeen is the third to slide left all or partway around a lake. The fairway narrows significantly on the approach. Two bunkers lie to the right 90 yards from the green, which is tucked away left. A front bunker is poised to catch second shots falling short. Arthur Hills is generous as ever with a bailout area; a gully lies to the right of the green.

A tree stands in the line of sight just off the eighteenth tee to the right. Left is safe play, right has a ribbon waste bunker with trees at this extremity of the hole. The fairway kicks right 50 yards from the green. A central ridge sheds balls left and right, and the surface angles forward.

Coming through the cordgrass, an ibis dots the ground hurriedly as if grabbing a snack on her way to work.

"Thank you for visiting with me today," I say, saluting my feathery friends.

Part II

Orlando Area

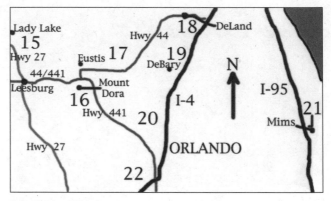

Orlando Area North

15 Harbor Hills
16 Mount Dora
17 Black Bear
18 Victoria Hills
19 DeBary
20 Wekiva
21 Walkabout
22 MetroWest

15

Harbor Hills Country Club

6538 Lake Griffin Road, Lady Lake 32159
(352) 753-7711
www.harborhills.com

Green fee: $55

Architects: Lloyd Clifton, Ken Ezell, and George Clifton, 1988
Par 72
Blue yardage 6,551; course rating 70.8; slope rating 125
Red yardage 5,351; course rating 70.3; slope rating 115

*Directions: Harbor Hills is in Lady Lake, north of 44 and east of 27. From
44 in Leesburg take 27 north for 8.5 miles. At Lemon Street turn right, go 0.1
miles, and at Lake Griffin Road turn left. In 4.6 miles, entrance (Clubhouse
Road) is on right.*

At the fourteenth, I'd been waiting a while behind a blind ridge for a foursome
of resident members to hole out. Approaching the brow, I discovered the coast
was clear. On getting closer I saw four balls lying on the green left there, I
first thought, by early-morning maintenance crews who rake bunkers and find
balls, setting them on view as gifts for dew sweepers. Then I spied a putter, and
another, in fact four putters. A golfing version of the *Marie Celeste*, found float-
ing with dinner prepared in the galley and the table set but nobody aboard.

Harbor Hills' clubhouse stands on one of the highest points in central Florida, with a gorgeous view over Lake Griffin. Elevation changes throughout the
round require a range of shot making, uphill and downhill off tees, in lies, and
into greens. Varied green shapes and bunkering make it a joy to play, challenging all departments of a player's game.

The 374-yard first hole slides left, with a hazard right of the broad landing
area. The raised, forward-sloping green is bunkered at both sides and backed
by a palm-planted mound. Number two is one yard shorter. The tee box points
right of center, the correct line in order to avoid a cross bunker at the 150-yard
marker. From this distance, as the ground gently rises, two large bunkers at the

Six—a strategist's hole.

rear of the green appear to be in front. In these cases I never know whether to applaud the architects or curse my optician.

The third falls downhill off the tee and draws left. Long hitters can try to carry the cross bunker but are forced to cut a second corner to reach the green on this 500-yarder. The safer play is out to the right, although this means coming in over greenside hazards. The putting surface falls away to the rear left. A beautifully strategic hole, this is where the architects do win the applause.

Six is a 498-yard par 5 and, again, a strategist's dream. The tee shot is directed into a valley with aiming bunkers to the right. The fairway tilts left on the second shot. A diagonal cross bunker covers the width of the approach from 100 yards. Treated as a three-shot hole, it has a bailout area at front left of the green, but still entails a carry over sand. The green has a horizontal ridge breaking left and right, and forward and backward.

On eight, a 169-yard par 3, the tee boxes point to the right of the pin, and the green slopes to the front left quarter. Four flashed bunkers cover the front, and a deep bunker runs rear at the right. The outward par 3s are dry, while the pair on the back nine are fronted by water—an infrequent feature at Harbor Hills. Thirteen looks innocuous at 171 yards, but the 5,200-square-foot target has front and rear bunkers and breaks subtly forward. The sixteenth is a longer carry, 185 yards, also with front hazards and a steep bank at the rear. Better to hit into the bank than the alligator pond.

The 406-yard ninth angles right, with bunkers at both sides of the apex. A front bunker, 12 yards off the green, might tempt the first-time visitor to under-club on approach. A mogul sits in the front half of the putting surface, which is framed on three sides by ribbon bunkers. This is rated hardest hole on the course.

I had read that Harbor Hills was near a ghost town, Slighville. Sam and Jake Sligh settled by Lake Griffin before the Civil War and ran the boat landing, a cotton gin, and the stagecoach line from Leesburg to Ocala. The community had its own post office until the coming of the railroad moved many residents to Lady Lake.

Before current development, Harbor Hills was a port of call for minitour events and U.S. Open qualifying rounds. Brady Godfrey, resident professional, sees the club eventually turning private. There is still time to enjoy the elegant redbrick Georgian-style clubhouse and perfectly manicured putting green. Yale University Endowment owns Harbor Hills; a fair-sized community en-compasses the course, although not all inhabitants are doctors or lawyers.

The tenth is a spectacular downhill play with water at left and two bunkers to the right. A ribbon trap runs left from 100 yards to a small green presided

Tenth green and clubhouse.

over by oak trees. Eleven and twelve complete a stout trio to start the back nine. Large oaks block the left side off the tee at the twelfth, and a sizeable fairway bunker lies to the right at driving distance.

The fifteenth drifts right and downhill. The green slopes away from the front left, and bunkers protect the right side. Seventeen shapes around a corner and uphill to the left. The unguarded green slopes from high left, as if propped up on one elbow. At the last, a 202-yard drive is necessary to clear a deep gully and find rising fairway. It's another 50 yards to carry bunkers on this 552-yard par 5. This fairway table drops forward into rough 130 yards from green center. The putting surface is triangled by sand hazards.

After my round, I spoke with Otto the ranger about the ghostly fourteenth green. Apparently one of the foursome had a cell phone call from his wife, who needed help to rid their house of a snake. All four men went gallantly to the rescue. After all, golf is only a game and not a matter of life and death . . . though some would say it's much more important than that.

Mount Dora Golf Club

1100 South Highland Street, Mount Dora 32757
(352) 383-3954

Green fee: $26

Architects: Clayton Tremain, 1945; additional nine by Harold Paddock, 1959
Par 70 (blue), 72 (red)
Blue yardage 5,719; course rating 67.3; slope rating 118
Red yardage 5,238; course rating 70.6; slope rating 118

*Directions: At the junction of 441 and 46 in Mount Dora, take 46 west 0.7
miles. At Old 441 South (South Highland Street) turn left. In 0.6 miles,
entrance is on left.*

"New England with alligators" is one popular description of the quaint little
town of Mount Dora. Such a community of restaurants, boutiques, and shops
selling antiques and curios would not be out of place in the Northeast. At
266 feet above sea level, for Florida it's Appalachian, but the winter crowd
would have to water-ski across the lake instead of downhill. Mount and lake
are named, some would have it, after a nineteenth-century resident, Dora
Drawdy, whose husband Jim must have enjoyed pulling bass and catfish from
the teeming water. The town's Lakeside Inn dates back to the late 1800s, and
President and Mrs. Coolidge recuperated here after he left office. For the 1981
comedy *Honky Tonk Freeway*, film director John Schlesinger had the whole
place painted pink.

If by chance you find yourself at the Country Club of Mount Dora, then
you're not in the place covered by this chapter. Mount Dora Golf Club, the
older of the two venues, is also posted as Mount Dora Golf Association.

Built at the end of World War II as a nine-hole course, it sits on a terrace
that drops away steeply; half the holes play into or out of the valley. Holes one
through four, nine, ten, and eighteen lie on the high table. The scorecard map
shows them stacked like pancakes. Perpendicular to the stack, the 299-yard
eighth hole runs from south to north. Nestled on either side lie two par 3s:
seven goes south, and eleven runs north. In the valley-side stack of holes, the

In and out of
the valley.

pancakes in the middle have shifted diagonally. Comprising most of the back nine plus five and six, these are the cardiac holes for walkers. The player inevitably plays second shots from an uneven lie and often has to hit up to go down, if you get my drift.

I arrived on the day of the men's skins game, difficult to miss as it takes place Wednesday through Saturday. Another group, the Raiders, precede the skins players in their own contest. At the end of the round, I was privy to healthy banter in the male-members-only clubroom. A few pennies changed hands here and there, and scissors snipped at handicaps of players who "played too good."

Brooks Barth is the head professional, with a background in the automobile industry. With his smooth southern delivery and gentle manners, I bet he cleared whole parking lots. Chuckling, he revealed he had turned pro only in his fifties. He's proudest of the fact he's the oldest working pro who ever had a heart transplant.

Mike "Cotton" Smith has been at Mount Dora his whole life and is scorekeeper for the skins game. He remembers, as a small boy, watching Clayton Tremain building the holes with a plough and a mule. An old couple used to collect him and another lad from school every day to shag balls for them. Cotton caddied here and so developed into a proficient player himself. He well recalls the routing of the old nine. The addition of nine holes by Harold Paddock in 1959 took away the driving range, although today a short-game practice area exists down in the valley holes.

Held for more than forty years, the club's annual three-day Invitational Tournament attracts a field of 156 amateurs with at least 90 single-digit handicappers. More recently the club has hosted the Jim Dennis Memorial, commemorating a golf shoe representative who did much to encourage the growth of the women's game. The winner in 2004 was In-Bee Park.

The opening holes play up and back to the clubhouse, with a par 3 following. The fourth tee provides dangerous entertainment—a duck hook will swing menacingly toward the third green. The fairway drifts to the right at about 175 yards from the green.

The fifth is where the valley drops in on the round. Playing 489 yards downhill, the fairway cants sharply left as if warped by the sun (see color plate 6). The sixth returns uphill to a plateau green. After the south-north combo of seven and eight, the ninth executes a little draw back to the clubhouse.

The twelfth, like five, plunges into the valley. When this was still a nine-hole track, it played all the way to the fifteenth green, the lowest part of the property. To reach today's twelfth green, 398 yards from the tee, requires a carry over a dainty island set within an ornamental pond.

At the one-shot thirteenth I met Ben Crunk, and we swapped family tales. I despaired of not having golfer's genes. He countered, "They gave me the Ben, but didn't give me the Crenshaw or the Hogan." Like Cotton Smith, he's a lifelong Mount Dora resident and helps out with the ground maintenance. "This is the kind of place where everybody knows everybody else, all the regulars. If you happen upon a club, a wedge by a bunker, say, you'll know who it belongs to."

Sixteen begins a long climb back to the eighteenth tee; two ponds impinge upon the play, off the tee and 275 yards distant. Waiting patiently on the tee box was a gentleman in his eighties who played for the University of Florida in 1937. "We had no scratch players; back then they used a ladder system and you played in turn. I was about a two or three, I guess." He introduced himself as Ernie Moore. His wiry figure still hits a straight ball—positively no relation to me. Clubhouse plaques record his holes-in-one: on eleven in 1993 and, the final ace of the 1900s, at thirteen on December 29, 1999. Definitely different genes.

17

Black Bear Golf Club

24505 Calusa Boulevard, Eustis 32736
(352) 357-4732

Green fee: $55

Architect: P. B. Dye, 1995
Par 72
Black yardage 6,394; course rating 71.6; slope rating 127
Green yardage 5,044; course rating 70.5; slope rating 121

Directions: From I-4 exit 101C, take 46 west 13.5 miles to 437 North. Turn right and go 4.9 miles. At 44A turn right, go 0.5 miles to Lake Norris Road, and turn left. Entrance (Calusa Boulevard) is on left in 0.3 miles.

From 441 in Mount Dora, take 46 east 4.7 miles to 437 North. Turn left and go 4.9 miles. At 44A turn right, go 0.5 miles to Lake Norris Road, and turn left. Entrance (Calusa Boulevard) is on left in 0.3 miles.

From 19 in Eustis, take 44 (Orange Avenue) east 8.1 miles to 437 North. Turn left and go 1.7 miles. At 44A turn right, go 0.5 miles to Lake Norris Road, and turn left. Entrance (Calusa Boulevard) is on left in 0.3 miles.

"Middle of nowhere," they said. "Keep going until you think you're lost, but then keep going and you're probably getting near us." If you drew a triangle between Orlando, Ocala, and Daytona Beach, Black Bear would be about at the center, perhaps a teensy bit closer to Orlando. The manager and assistant professional take impromptu mileages when traveling, and phone them in. Folks from The Villages, guys from Daytona Beach, and people from Orlando are the most frequent visitors. The staff ensure you CAN get there from here, which is just east of Eustis, and then left, right, and left again . . .

Waiting for you are a moonscape of pot bunkers and large greenside capes, turf stretched tight as baize over a billiard table, and the odd tree strategically placed here and there. Be prepared for a lot of bump and roll rather than bump and run where you have a general idea of the line. On fairways of wild undulation the ball speeds along most certainly heading for a gully or a bunker.

Turf pulled tight like baize.

Greens are deep and narrow; many contain mounds spilling to a goodly variety of cupping areas.

There is no doubt that I missed seeing this course in its virgin state. The lack of development in its first decade let it age, and acquire a great reputation. A flurry of construction began in 2005, as the original owner bought back the course that had been held in stasis by previous management. Houses will undeniably change the outlook. But Black Bear sits on the ground so harmonically that the addition of vertical elements at the sides of fairways should not overly queer the pitch.

A Hooters Senior Tour event was under way at Black Bear during my visit. With the first threesome already away, I whisked the cart down the first, which plays into a valley, and to a punchbowl green with tall mounding. Bunkers look large here. Two has a thin strip of fairway to the right; the left undulates toward a gully strewn with pot bunkers. At the 250-yard marker more cavernous hazards lie left and a ribbon of bunkers to the right. The fairway's pattern switches over, with gully to the right on approach and the left becoming the high ground. Two pots at the left guard the green entrance; the narrow putting surface has a bump at center left. And yes, that was a par 5.

The green at the next, a par 3, is 42 yards deep by 14 yards wide. A front left pot and two craters to the right demand pinpoint accuracy off the tee. The putting surface falls away to the rear from a front left mound. Hole five is similar, with the green gathering this time in a bowl at center right.

A cul-de-sac of trees frames the approach on eight. Two bunkers sit at the right-side landing area, and a deep pot is placed left, 50 yards from the target. The green sheds from a mound at front right with a trio of pots behind.

On nine, staggered trees require precision for the player to reach the narrow landing area. The fairway opens up into moonscape. A peppering of pots covers the approach, and the green is surrounded by an amphitheater of mounds. Cream on the cake is a front right bunker that lifts the green as though picking up the edge of a carpet.

The tenth hole slips into a valley. Steep mounding to the right has a pot bunker in nearly every fold. The left greenside drops off into a deep bunker; a grass hollow protects the other side. This deep green cants to left front and center right. The view from the twelfth tee reminded me of the first at Royal County Down, playing up into a valley, but with a more forgiving landing area. Bunkers sit 25 yards from the green center. The elevated green has pots on both sides and a false front.

The tree covers the right approach.

The landing area shelf on thirteen runs between the 200- and 100-yard markers. Large shallow bunkers cover the left, and mounding to the right decreases in height, a single pine tree covering the right approach. A gully runs before the green, and deep bunkers guard the rear. Fourteen rocks and rolls 549 yards to a bench-terrace green tucked away at left. Bunkers flank the fairway throughout.

Sixteen doglegs right, tempting strong players to pass hazards on both shots to get on the dance floor in two. The softer way to catch this bear is three shots of honey. Cross bunkers cover the second landing area from the 150-yard marker. A wee gully, running laterally to the right near the green, gives a good placement to leave a short third shot.

Seventeen's tee shot is hit to a split fairway: a high shelf left or a thin ribbon below to the right. The green complex is elevated and forward sloping. A massive collection bunker lies to the right of the putting surface. Anything over the back of the green is gone, down and down to the eighteenth tee box.

Situated between Seminole and Ocala State Forests, this is truly black bear country. Manager Rafe Kirian was cashing up in the pro shop one Thanksgiving evening when he saw a bear peering through the shop window. Rafe thought Steve, the mechanic, had dressed up and was playing a joke. Some days later a local resident came in with a photograph of a black bear taken in his garden that very Thanksgiving afternoon.

Victoria Hills Golf Club

300 Spalding Way, DeLand 32724
(386) 738-6000
www.arvida.com/victoriapark/golf.asp

Green fee: $95

Architect: Ron Garl, 2001
Par 72
Gold yardage 6,495; course rating 71.8; slope rating 136
Green yardage 5,500; course rating 72.8; slope rating 129

Directions: From I-4 exit 116, take 4116 (Orange Camp Road) west 1.0 miles. At 4101 (Dr. Martin Luther King Jr. Beltway) turn left. In 0.3 miles, at Spalding Way, turn right; entrance is ahead.

From I-4 exit 114, take 472 west 0.6 miles. At 4101 (Dr. Martin Luther King Jr. Beltway) turn right. In 1.3 miles, at Spalding Way, turn left; entrance is ahead.

Ron Garl attended the University of Florida studying turfgrass science on the first golf scholarship ever granted by the Florida State Golf Association. Since graduating in 1967, he has been designing and building golf courses from his Lakeland office. Although the American designs of Donald Ross and Alister MacKenzie made the biggest impression on him, he cites Joe Lee and Dick Wilson as his local Florida influences. He considers Pine Valley and Augusta National the finest courses in America; across the Atlantic, it's Royal Birkdale, Turnberry, and Prestwick.

Early Garl shows an absence of waste areas, flatter fairways, and no amoebic bunkering. The work is formal, functional, and attractive in a fundamental way, but not flamboyant. Somewhere along the line, like an artist moving from charcoal to oils, a transition occurred and Ron Garl became vibrantly creative.

His fairways rise and fall, in a cupped shape that Garl calls the Good Hands. Mounding, waste areas planted with native grasses, and liberally sized bunkering are done with full, bold strokes of his brush. Lighter touches include use of crescent-shaped spurs grown with cordgrass, a hazard where otherwise a

Elaborate bunkering on three.

bunker might sit. Victoria Hills runs the gamut of bunker shapes and sizes; mounded clusters inhabit landing areas where early Garl would have placed a pair of flashed sand hazards. Greens are writ large in size and slope.

The Garl design team includes nephew Ricky Nix, who's been working with Ron since this explosion of exuberance. Steve McFarlane, from Troon, Scotland, is another associate. Plans are on the table for an indoor eighteen-hole course as part of an enormous development proposed for Memphis, Tennessee. In China, where the game is rocketing in popularity, a coastal layout includes a man-made peninsula to bring an island into the routing. Courses in Costa Rica and Thailand expand the team's portfolio.

Victoria Hills is Garl's sonnet to the pastoral. This golfing sonnet has fourteen holes, plus a couple of couplets. A rugged waste area off the first tee prepares the player for a visual feast; the fairway rumbles along between pines to an elevated, undulating green. A sandy mound planted with cordgrass sits 15 yards off the green to the right, and a bunker lies front left.

The second is a hit of 152 yards over a sprawling lace-edged bunker. The putting surface feeds to the front left. Forward tees are arranged to leave less obstacle to clear. From tee to green the third is 349 yards straight, but trees and bunkers cross the line of approach. The fairway rolls downhill to the right and into a field of bunkers. The green sits on a terrace; sitting below are sand hazards and crescent-shaped spurs of cordgrass, giving the impression of an inverted bunker with hair.

Four follows the landscape downhill to the widest part of the fairway at the 150-yard marker. The lakeside green is a picture postcard: it could be Scotland, North Carolina, or Maine. Next a spectacular par 3 plays over water and the forward tees to a raised green 210 yards distant (see color plate 7). Surrounding trees affect the perspective, bringing it closer. The putting surface slopes to the left, with a cant to the front left quarter.

Six forces play over and around a lake to the left in par-5 mode and is rated hardest hole. Mounding to the right carries the outer curve of the fairway. A bunker covers the right half of the angled green; another hazard waits at the rear.

The seventh is a devotional hole: the way up is short, but twists and turns from side to side and camber to camber. The green slopes toward you as you climb up the canyon. Nine has cross bunkers running from fairway center diagonally to the right. A large waste area dominates the midsection. Nine's green is my candidate for most difficult putting surface on this course.

Ten runs downhill to the left to avoid a waste feature. Bunkers occupy both sides of the 150-yard marker as the fairway continues tumbling left. The green is on a shelf to the right with one bunker and a front left pot.

Fourteen is a majestic hole and will surely win plaudits as one of the best in the state. A par 5 of 558 yards (581 from the champion tee), it has staggered bunker clusters on mounds left, then right, at the first landing zone. From here a waste area runs to the left for 80 yards as the fairway tilts and warps its way to the green complex. The green is bunkered at the rear and front right, and allows ground entry only from the left; the putting surface slopes to that quarter.

The eighteenth is a par 5 of 530 yards with a long carry over a waste area from the tee. Bunkers take the right side until 275 yards from the green. The land drops to the 150-yard marker where a spectacular bunkered mound stands to the right. A last spur of cordgrass and one greenside bunker cover the approach.

With its toughness from the champion tees, its visual beauty, and practice facilities of the sort one expects from an upscale venue, it's no surprise it has already held USGA Junior Match Play and PGA Senior Tour Qualifying events, and a U.S. Open Qualifier in 2006. Deland's Stetson University chose Victoria Hills as its home course. After thirty years in the business, Ron Garl is one of the deans of his profession. Victoria Hills is his Academe.

DeBary Golf and Country Club

300 Plantation Club Drive, DeBary 32713
(386) 668-1705
www.debarycc.com

Green fee: $75

Architects: Lloyd Clifton, Ken Ezell, and George Clifton, 1990
Par 72
White yardage 6,234; course rating 70.2; slope rating 130
Red yardage 5,060; course rating 69.4; slope rating 119

Directions: From I-4 exit 104, take 17 North [92 East] (Charles Richard Beall Boulevard) 5.2 miles. At DeBary Plantation Boulevard turn left and go 0.3 miles to Plantation Club Drive. Turn left; entrance is ahead.

From I-4 exit 111, take 4146 West (Saxon Boulevard) 1.9 miles to 17 South [92 West] (Charles Richard Beall Boulevard). Turn left and go 0.6 mile. At DeBary Plantation Boulevard turn right and go 0.3 miles to Plantation Club Drive. Turn left; entrance is ahead.

A resident recalls seeing deer on the DeBary golf course when it first opened. Another member once saw a black bear sauntering across the fifteenth fairway. Much of the wildlife has moved to pastures new since estate development began, but generations ago such animals drew people to this region and factored into the naming of the town.

Baron Samuel Frederick DeBary was born in Germany and came to America in 1840 as an agent for Mumm champagne and importer of other fine wines. From his New York office in those thriving days of Astors and Vanderbilts, DeBary indulged his passion for hunting. Enticed to Lake Monroe by the Brock House Hotel and deer, bear, raccoon, turkey, duck, and partridge, DeBary befriended the owner and sought local property. Construction of DeBary Hall was completed in 1871 and served as the family home for nearly one hundred years. In 1967 it became the headquarters of Florida's Federation of Art, and it now operates as gallery and museum.

The DeBary clubhouse has succeeded the old mansion in the role of center of community activity. Hunter's breakfast at 4:30 a.m. is not yet a fixture, although early morning tee times, banquets, weddings, and tennis and golf tournaments are all arranged here. As it is the focal point of a development, one expects housing around the fairways; however, the overriding impression is a country village setting.

Lloyd Clifton's design relies on subtle changes of elevation to create a variety of challenges for the golfer. Some holes have a tee shot into a valley and then an approach to a raised target. Others play uphill to a shelf and down into the green. Simple, formal bunkering is strategic and never superfluous. The final greens of the two nines sit back to back below the clubhouse on the fringe of a small lake.

Starting with the hardest hole, and a par 5 to boot, suggests the nines were reversed—which they were. The green, not visible from the tee, is tucked away 491 yards to the left on a terrace guarded by bunkers. The following par 3 goes uphill with bunkers front and rear. The third's tee boxes point to the right. The fairway is raised at the landing area and bunkered at both sides, 100 yards from the target. A big cape bunker covers the left front; the rear right shelf delivers to a cupping area at center left.

Seven, an attractive one-shot.

Eighteen's green before it was raised four feet.

The fourth tee shot favors a fade. An aiming bunker sits 220 yards away as the fairway elbows right. A deep hollow occupies the right side between the 200- and 150-yard markers. The second shot plays downhill, with a bunker covering the approach. The green slopes left to right and front to back.

Five plays uphill to bunkers on both sides of the landing area, then down to an attractive green complex. The ground falls away to the left where pine trees define the edge of the fairway. A front left bunker guards the green, which slopes to the front right quarter.

The sixth is a par 5 angling right. A drive of 230 yards should stay on the upper shelf, leaving 280 yards to the flag. Beyond, the ground dips toward a young pine tree covering the right approach at the 150-yard marker. A narrow entry to the green exists on the left; the right is covered by a deep sand hazard. Two bunkers sit behind the elevated green.

Seven is a photogenic par 3. Playing downhill 160 yards, the runway is hipped by mounding, and a greenside bunker waits to the left. A wide chipping area lies to the right; this is the place, if anywhere, to miss the target.

Eight's ideal tee shot should fade up the hill. The landing area is narrowed by sand hazards on both sides. The punchbowl green has a deep bunker to the right from where the land drops away steeply. Ten plays over wetland to an undulating fairway. The comfort zone is attained by a 215-yard drive finding a flat landing area, to leave 150 yards remaining. More undulations on the approach and a sand hazard block the right side of the green. The eleventh doglegs left. Staggered patches of rough and hollows form the center of the fairway. Bunkers fore and aft protect the wide, forward-pitching green.

Tall pines provide the backdrop for the par-3 twelfth. A gully runs vertically through the green at center left. Fourteen and fifteen remain good holes despite the addition of new homes. The former slides right, with ground falling away left on the approach. A deep bunker left of the green forces the higher, right-sided way in. The sand behind is an obvious compatible hazard. Fifteen is straight, with a ribbon bunker lying to the left. Trees constrict the second shot, calling for either great height or accuracy with a low bump and run. Measuring only 340 yards, this is an attractive and testing short par 4 and one of my favorites in the Orlando area.

Sixteen is the ideal longest-drive hole since markers in the fairway denote distance off the tee. A companion plaque on this par 5 commemorates one member who covered 400 yards in two shots in the club championship; he took another sixteen strokes to complete the hole.

The eighteenth doglegs right, with an approach, like nine's, downhill to the lakeside green. Formerly their situation at water level made them prone to flooding and receptively soggy. Both greens have been raised four feet. Now reaching prouder, possibly harder surfaces will be like hitting onto a tambourine instead of a wet blanket. Construction was delayed in early 2005 to allow a baby crane to reach maturity. Sandhill cranes nest near the final hole, their chicks a fragile delight every spring. I'm sure Baron DeBary would have left them well alone.

Wekiva Golf Club

200 Hunt Club Boulevard, Longwood 32779
(407) 862-5113
www.wekivagolfclub.com

Green fee: $55

Architect: Ward Northrup, 1975
Par 72
Back yardage 6,640; course rating 71.9; slope rating 123
Forward yardage 5,735; course rating 73.2; slope rating 126

*Directions: From I-4 exit 94, go west on 434 for 0.9 miles. At Wekiva Springs
Road turn right, go 3.3 miles to N Hunt Club Boulevard, and turn left. In 1.2
miles, at Wekiva Club Court, turn right; entrance is ahead.*

It's a rare father who'll build a golf course as a practice facility solely for his
daughter. Tammy Bowman was the lucky girl back in 1972; her father, Kayo,
purchased land in Longwood for a song. Ward Northrup designed the front
nine, and the eighteen-hole layout officially opened three years later. To show
her appreciation, Tammy worked diligently and peaked as one of the top amateurs of her day. A golf property management company made the Bowmans
an offer, and it ceased to be a family affair. Once the real estate was sold, the
rose lost its bloom.

As bees buzz to new flowers, the turn of the millennium saw a change of
fortune at Wekiva. The management company decided to liquidate its golfing
assets. In an orderly ongoing fashion, twenty-nine of thirty-four properties
were sold in three years. A new owner purchased Wekiva in 2004. An industri-
ous staff, dedicated to the inspired independent interest, has life looking rosy
again for this golf club.

The new regime has upgraded and lengthened Wekiva. It was already one
of the longest ladies' courses in Orlando from the forward tees. With wide
fairways, simple bunker shapes, and greens of subtle undulation, it was as
unashamedly 1970s as bellbottoms, double albums, and 8-track tapes. "Somewhere easy to post a good score," some might think, but this game defies scorn.

One member of the staff, a single-digit handicapper, scored 73 one day and 88 the next. The trio around the turn, as well as holes fourteen, fifteen, and seventeen, are good tests of dead aim.

A bunker at the left landing area leaves 200 yards to go at the par-4 first. The approach is downhill, the green bunkered at both sides with a small ridge running from left center. The tee shot at number two also plays downhill, with cross bunkers and trees covering the left-hand side. Two bunkers catch anything wide and right, 125 to 85 yards from the green. A pair of pot bunkers sits greenside right, one deep bunker to the left, and another hazard at the rear. A vertical ridge runs from the back of the putting surface. Suddenly posting a good score seems not so simple.

At the par-5 third, trouble lies on the approach: from the 200-yard marker, a gully runs into water to the left. The teardrop green is framed on three sides by shallow bunkers. Four is a one-shot to an angled green, sloping to the front. Staggered bunkers lie 220 yards off the tee at the fifth. A sand hazard guards the front left of the target. The sixth is a 155-yard par 3, played uphill to a green protected on three sides and a narrow runway entrance.

A school across the way and constant everyday activity on surrounding roads gives Wekiva Springs a long-lived-in feeling. Before Kayo Bowman

A long-lived-in feeling.

Seventeen's carry looking back from the well-guarded green.

built the course, there was nothing here. The Seminole, however, used aquifer springs hereabouts. European settlers soon discovered the water source for themselves. In the early twentieth century a Swedish community farmed celery in nearby Sanford, using grids of irrigation tiles long before they were used under golf courses. Sanford became Celery City, the world's leading producer. In 1909 a crate of celery fetched $1.25; eight hundred crates came from one acre; 209 acres were in production. By 1923, six thousand acres were cultivated. Three years later, celery was an $8 million crop before the ruinous depression caused local bank failure.

The par-5 ninth elbows uphill to the left. Cross bunkers cover the left landing area, and bunkers on both sides lie 75 yards from the green. The two-tier putting surface flows from rear left to front right. Ten has staggered bunkers at both landing areas and a field of bunkers before the small green. The eleventh doglegs left, with two bunkers and a tree guarding the inner angle 200 yards from the pin.

Fourteen has one of the narrower fairways, with mounds to the right. A bunker lies left, 225 yards from the green, which is guarded by sand on both sides. On the 499-yard dogleg fifteenth, the fairway is only 18 yards wide at the 250-yard marker. Bunkers are placed at both sides of the apex; two trees to the left hinder second shots. More hazards lie 100 yards from a small green bunkered on all sides.

The picturesque seventeenth features a penal 160-yard carry over water to a tiny green ringed by sand hazards. A live oak shuts the door on approach from the left. The home hole curls around a lake to the right. The green is well protected, with a narrow entrance at front left.

Longwood's name lends itself to a corny golf connotation, but the town's Big Tree Park is all it suggests. The Senator grows here, the largest cypress tree in the United States, more than three thousand years old, 126 feet tall, and nearly 18 feet in diameter. The tree's age is not the source of the town name. Longwood was named by founder Edward Warren Henck, a member of the honor guard on the train taking Lincoln's body from Washington to Illinois. He helped build Longwood Estate in Brookline, Massachusetts, for David Sears, a Boston merchant. Sears had visited Paris in 1813 and later named his estate Longwood after Napoleon Bonaparte's home in exile on St. Helena. What bizarre bubbles of knowledge spring from Wekiva surroundings.

One of the senior lady members offered something more up-to-date: "Tell them we call some of the trees now by different names! Since the hurricanes whipped through, we've got 'hangers' and 'leaners'—and some 'hangers that lean.'"

Walkabout Golf and Country Club

3230 Folsom Road, Mims 32754
(321) 385-2099
www.walkaboutgolf.com

Green fee: $60

Architect: Perry Dye, 2003
Par 72
Blue yardage 6,123; course rating 69.3; slope rating 127
Red yardage 4,873; course rating 69.1; slope rating 127

Directions: From I-95 exit 223, go east on 46 for 0.2 miles to entrance on left.

Perry O'Neal Dye is part of the great Dye golf-designing dynasty. Parents Pete and Alice O'Neal Dye are responsible for bringing an authentic Scottish feel to American courses after their sojourn in the cradle of golf in the early 1960s. Railroad ties, majestic sod-faced bunkers, and a prevalence of sand are now established as the "primary colors" of an architect's palette. Perry is the older brother of P. B. (Paul Burke) Dye, who was always more likely to wear a designer's hat. Perry studied at the University of Denver, ventured into real estate, then returned to the family calling. Walkabout is a return to his adolescent stamping ground: as a teenager he helped with the routing of John's Country Club in Vero Beach, a two-hour drive down the Atlantic coast.

Jan Stephenson is the Australian firecracker of women's golf. Winning the Australian Open in 1973 after an impressive junior career, she joined the LPGA as Rookie of the Year in 1974. Three majors and a clutch of other titles give her the right to voice opinions, which has earned her a reputation as outspoken. She promoted the Women's Senior Golf Tour in 2004 by playing with the men on the Champions Tour in Hawaii. Her stamp on the course is more than the kangaroo logo. Stephenson made over 50 visits to the course during its construction, working closely with architect Perry Dye.

The word "walkabout" describes an Aborigine's return home from working in white society, usually involving a journey through the bush. Walkabout's course meanders through wetland with little natural elevation change. Wind

Dye's coffin.

must be considered an ever-present factor. Water is a lateral hazard on two-thirds of the track, with only a handful of forced carries. Bunkers are painted with a broad brush. Green sizes vary anywhere from 4,500 to 7,500 square feet.

The first throws itself right around a lake with two beach bunkers at the underbelly of the hole. A generous fairway curls around to the 100-yard marker, then into a green with water at front right and a bunker front left. The runways are Tifdwarf, normally used on greens, giving a welcome entrance along the ground.

Two, as I look at the scorecard, resembles a fish. The fairway has a widening shaped like a dorsal fin at the first landing area; the second landing area

Bunkered mound covers entry on sixteen.

is much tighter, with bunkers on both sides. The one-shot third is penal in triplicate: a carry over wetland, lake, and front bunker to a receptive green.

The hogsback fairway at the 404-yard fourth lies to the right of the tee boxes and over water. The landing area has a central ridge dispersing balls toward water at left or rough to right. At the 150-yard marker, the fairway flattens out to narrow considerably at the 100-yard marker. The green is 40 yards deep by 18 yards wide and sheds rear right and front left.

An aerial view of the sixth resembles the profile of an angelfish. The fairway widens to a corner on the right, where a cape bunker mimics pouting lips. The approach plays over water to a green guarded in front by a 70-yard-long ribbon bunker. The hole is drivable all the way over water, 314 yards from the blue tees.

Number eight plays over wetland, a 177-yard carry off the tee to a rising shelf of fairway. A long, shallow hazard gathers anything right up to 90 yards from green center. The open target has one pot bunker below center left.

The ninth really does look like the head and neck of a racehorse in full stride, I'm not kidding. The lake off the tee is the cheek and lower jaw. The water, running left of the fairway for the remainder of the hole, is the horse's flowing mane. The forward tee box is the left eye. The right side of the hole holds a multitude of hazards. First is a large collection bunker; out-of-bounds runs the rest of the way, while a stand of live oaks and a lone cabbage palm cover the right, 175 yards from the green. A bunker lies at the 100-yard marker, with one placed greenside for good measure.

On the back nine I tried to concentrate on the golf instead of this bestiary of dreamtime. A more pragmatic philosophy stems from Alice Dye's paper "It's Time to Move Forward," regarding the Two Tee System of optimum length of courses: 5,800 yards for women and 6,400 yards for men.

Three holes beginning at the twelfth run along the eastern perimeter, with prevailing wind from behind. To the right off the tee, mounds and bunkers line the 420-yard twelfth. From the 150-yard marker, this effect is repeated to the left with some playful bunker shapes. A deep green with a high point at center left sheds balls front and rear. A collection bunker waits at front right. Thirteen is a par 5 with a 50-yard-long ribbon cape to the right from the 250-yard marker. A deep sand hazard sits greenside left.

Fourteen is a 370-yard par 4. Water runs all the way left until the 100-yard marker, where a tall mound covered with cordgrass takes over. The one-shot fifteenth plays 120 yards over water to a raised putting table. Bunkers stand guard all round, with a coffin bunker at front center.

Only 278 yards long, sixteen is a "beaut," as an Australian might say. Trees block the left side off the tee. To the right, at the 100-yard marker, a large mound with bunkers inhibits view of the target. Two front pots guard the green, one barely big enough to accommodate a sheep. Beside this hole in the hardwood wetland stands an eagle's nest high in a tree. In early April the fledglings were stretching their wings. The nineteenth, a playoff hole, plays 75 yards over water to a green shaped like Australia, reminding us of Jan Stephenson's origins.

22

MetroWest Golf Club

2100 Hiawassee Road, Orlando 32835
(407) 299-1099
www.metrowestgolf.com

Green fee: $129

Architect: Robert Trent Jones Sr., 1987
Par 72
Blue yardage 6,619; course rating 71.1; slope rating 130
Red yardage 5,325; course rating 70.3; slope rating 122

Directions: From I-4 exit 75B, take 435 North (Kirkman Road) 2.8 miles. At MetroWest Boulevard go left 1.0 miles to Hiawassee Road. Turn left, go 0.3 miles to Lake Debra Drive, and turn right; entrance is ahead.

From 408 Expressway exit 4, go south on Hiawassee Road 2.4 miles. At Lake Debra Drive turn right; entrance is ahead.

MetroWest embodies the practical philosophy to which modern developers should aspire. This is no gated or closed community; it's an open enclave, its formal character signifying order and cleanliness and well-being. The idea behind MetroWest is similar to the Internationalist vision that architects in the 1920s and 1930s built between bouts of economic depression and before man's obsession with war stunted its further development.

MetroWest, the golf course, runs in two out-and-back loops, south then west, with over 100 feet in elevation change. Water influences play on only six holes. Bunkers, seventy-nine by my count, are large and free-form, with no fairway or green unprotected. Chosen as an annual site for U.S. Open Qualifying since 1999 and for the Champions Tour Qualifying since 1997, the venue hosted the Florida State Amateur in 2003 and is a regular award-winner on "best" lists.

In the tradition of a forgiving opening, 370 yards rise slightly as two bunkers press into the left side of the fairway landing area. A teardrop green, narrower at the rear, is guarded on both sides, more crucially in front by a pot bunker.

Nine, where John Daly drove the green 328 yards across water.

The second is a touch longer, with more trouble off the tee for the wayward drive. After a short chute, water and out-of-bounds lie left and a big banana slice can find water to the right. For the longer, straight hitter a ribbon bunker sits right at driving distance. The green is T-shaped and falls to the front; bunkers guard both sides.

Three is a one-shot to a three-tiered putting surface. Spreading, free-form hazards sit off the green enough to leave a decent collar. The fourth, rated hardest hole, is also the longest at 568 yards. An ample bunker cluster covers the right side of the first landing area, and a mature oak takes the left just beyond. The fairway doglegs right at the second landing area, with sand hazards on both sides of the approach. The elevated green has formidable bunkers below on the right, further inhibiting a two-shot play.

The 388-yard fifth slides right; again, bunkers squeeze the fairway at driving distance, although Trent Jones allows enough room for shorter strikes. The target is triangled by sand. Six, of similar length, ups the ante in difficulty. A large bunker to the left must be carried to create optimum position for the second shot. Missing the hazard to the right means a longer approach from an awkward lie. A deep bunker left of center guards the raised, stepped green, which flows to the front right quarter.

Seven is a 517-yard three-shot, with a tight fairway lined by trees in the mid-section. Number eight is your chance to win $5,000 by scoring an ace of 150 yards or more. Two bunkers protect the front of the green, and one the rear. A pole-mounted camera broadcasts play to the pro shop. The chances are about one in twenty thousand, and the winnings afford another thirty-five rounds of golf, allowing for the customary celebratory beverages.

The ninth runs all the way around a lake to the left. A plaque on the gold tee records the distance to the center of the green, 328 yards, and the feat of John Daly: with a mammoth drive, he cleared the water and landed his ball on the green. For those of us whose play matches the temper of hickory and Haskell, the dry route to the right is safer.

Ten is no breather at 540 yards. The fairway tilts right as it nears the target, and a line of free-form bunkers blankets the right approach all the way to the elevated green complex. The eleventh is a short par 4. A ribbon of water runs right off the tee to the landing area, where bunkers crowd the fairway at both sides. The ridged green, its left half sitting higher, is triangled by sand hazards.

Two par 4s of around 370 yards and medium difficulty follow. Twelve is pretty; a lake frames the entire left side, with a sparse stand of oaks at the midsection. A fairway bunker lies opposite, and another guards the greenside front left. The green (see color plate 8), nearly cloverleaf in shape, flows from rear left; the front right lobe is the lowest portion. The thirteenth tee sits atop a high knoll behind twelve's green. Looking back eastward affords a marvelous view of metropolitan Orlando and the city center's high-rise buildings.

Fourteen, a 529-yard par 5, is rated hardest hole on this side. Bunkers take the left landing area for short and long drives. The ground tumbles forward on the latter half of the approach, and the green sits on a peninsula jutting into the lake.

Fifteen and seventeen are par 3s. The first measures 161 yards, with water at left that cuts in front of the target. A big bunker covers greenside right on both holes, and two pots block the entrance to seventeen's green. The tee shot requires a carry over a pond and wetland creek to reach the target 198 yards away.

Trees line the right of the home fairway until the landing area, where a bunker lies left. The deep and narrow green has two sand hazards to the left, but water takes greenside right in ominous fashion.

I developed a crush on MetroWest over a courtship of four visits. So clean and simple in line, it has the appearance of a garden suburb course from the 1930s, and an established neighborhood adds weight to this impression of age. Searching for analogies, I thought it would be an apt setting for a P. G. Wodehouse comedy or an Agatha Christie murder mystery. If MetroWest were a car, it would be a Cadillac. If it were a meal, it would be chateaubriand and a bottle of Burgundy, citrus-scented cheesecake, and a glass of port. If this course were a person, it would be Grace Kelly or Fred Astaire. In a word, it's classy.

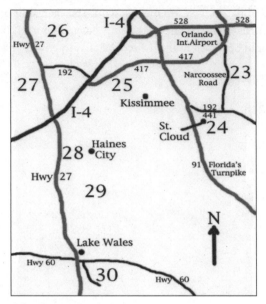

Orlando Area South

23

Eagle Creek Golf Club

10350 Emerson Lake Boulevard, Orlando 32827
(407) 273-4653
www.eaglecreekgolf.info

Green fee: $120

Architects: Ron Garl and Harold Swan, 2004
Par 73
Yellow yardage 6,407; course rating 70.4; slope rating 122
Red yardage 5,324; course rating 69.4; slope rating 124

*Directions: From 417 (Central Florida GreeneWay) exit 22, go south on
Narcoossee Road 1.9 miles; entrance is on left.*

Sitting on Narcoossee Road about 6,500 yards and a wedge away from prestigious Lake Nona, Eagle Creek will get its core business from its own upscale property development. Located close to Orlando International Airport and mindful of golfing tourists, it adopted "Save the best 'til last!" as its opening campaign slogan. I trust this remains a permanent rally.

The first event held on Emerson Lake Boulevard was a charity tournament for Arnold Palmer's Children's Hospital. A progressive Anglo-American cooperation has produced a track worthy of both tournament and recreational play. In Lakeland's Ron Garl and Englishman Harold Swan we see the marriage of true minds, and their collaboration displays a melding of styles, undoubtedly Orlando yet with European embellishments: The terrain is flat, the tee boxes are square. Waste areas are a local influence; sod-revetted bunkers owe more to Scotland.

The front nine circles in two clockwise loops at the front of the property, first south, then north of the clubhouse. It starts quietly with an easing-in hole of 326 yards. A bunker to the right gives the line to the green; more hazards sit left at the 100-yard marker. A simple bunker lies far enough off the green, leaving a sufficient collar for the player to hit confidently into the forward-sloping putting surface. The second is a short par 4 of 312 yards. A pair of mounded bunkers, 200 yards off the tee to the right, must be cleared. From there, water

An Anglo-American blend.

runs to the left. The green complex is raised and mounded at the rear. The putting surface slopes from rear right to front left.

The third has a sizeable waste area surrounding the tee boxes. Two prongs of sand jut forward to frame the fairway, which rises to a shelf 150 to 110 yards from the target. Bunkers cover the approach. At 522 yards, the fourth has staggered bunkers right and then left of the first landing area. The fairway snakes on the approach, with a cross bunker to the right and a lake to the left. A huge lace-edged bunker sits below the green's left.

Five is a one-shot hole played over a pair of pot bunkers 70 yards off the green; they look like nostrils to me. The computer graphic of the fifth plainly resembles a bull's head, even though one of the chief designers insists otherwise. The undulating green has a receptive area at center right.

Six is the toughest hole at Eagle Creek. Played over water, a 180-yard drive should clear a long ribbon bunker at the entrance to the fairway. Grass hollows and pot bunkers guard the green to the right. The putting surface flows from a hump at center left. The seventh doglegs right over water, and two bunkers are placed at the inner angle. On the course plan these bunkers look suspiciously like the letters EC.

The 172-yard eighth features a comic garden bunker, the sort of display one sees at horticultural shows, only in play from the back tees. Despite this distraction, the green matches the links style with a single, deep pot bunker to the right, meant to echo the Road Hole bunker at St. Andrews.

The back nine wends around the interior of the property to the far southeast corner shared by fourteen's green and fifteen's tees. Ten doglegs left, with the tee shot aimed over water and between two bunkers 220 yards from the yellow tees. A mid-iron approach remains to a forward-sloping green with sand hazard at left and grass hollow to the right. The thirteenth also doglegs left, measuring 484 yards. Three pot bunkers wait left of the first landing area and a cape bunker to the right. A line of three cross bunkers eats into the right side of the fairway 135 to 95 yards out.

Fourteen's fairway rises to a ridge with sand at both sides 180 yards from the target. On the downhill approach, a necklace of bunkers surrounds the green, lying on a bald mound.

The next hole also wears its hazards like jewelry, namely a decorative waste area off the tee. A carry of 150 yards straight reaches the fairway. Bunkers sit 220 yards from the tee to the right and one 50 yards farther to the left. Sand fronts the green on both sides.

Aim at the clubhouse clock.

Island tee boxes at sixteen, complete with bulkheads, are a nice touch. This par 5 has a large cross bunker to the right 130 yards from the flag. The putting surface slopes to front left. Seventeen is a scenic par 3 played over water to the bulkhead green. Pots front and rear guard the left side; a cape lies to the right. A crescent-shaped spur of cordgrass, a Garl feature, frames the right side of the hole.

The eighteenth was designed as a par 4, but the owners saw potential in having the green closer to the clubhouse. The green was accordingly moved back behind a water hazard to make a fifth par 5 and 73 par for the course. Cross bunkers cover the left at driving distance, and a lake with a ribbon beach bunker lies to the right. The second-shot choice is to lay up to wedge distance or to attempt to fly the water. Aim at the clubhouse clock; this approach works at the best of venues.

Royal St. Cloud Golf Links

5310 Michigan Avenue, St. Cloud 34772
(407) 891-7010
www.stcloudgolfclub.com

Green fee: $64

Architect: Chip Powell, 2001
Par 72
Gold yardage 6,680; course rating 72.2; slope rating 125
Citrus yardage 5,531; course rating 71.2; slope rating 115

*Directions: In St. Cloud, the club is located on Michigan Avenue 2.6 miles south
of the junction with 192 East [441 South] (13th Avenue).*

*From 91 (Florida's Turnpike) South exit 244, take 192 East [441 South] 5.6
miles.*

*From 91 (Florida's Turnpike) North exit 242, take 192 East [441 South] 3.7
miles.*

*Michigan Avenue is 2.0 miles west of Narcoossee Road, or 11.4 miles south of
exit 22 of 417 (Central Florida GreeneWay), or 15.2 miles south of exit 13 of 528
(Bee Line Expressway).*

Where else to hold a British Junior Amateur Championship in June but Royal
St. Cloud? A mini claret jug goes to the winner of the three-day event, not to
be confused with the official British Boys Open run by the Royal and Ancient
Golf Club. Nick Dougherty, protégé of Nick Faldo, practiced here regularly in
the winter before his 2005 win at the Singapore Masters on the European Tour.
An English-style pub and clubhouse is on the drawing board and a nine-hole
expansion on the cards. Each nine will be renamed after a famous course. If
these should happen to be Muirfield, St. Andrews, and Augusta, they'd reveal
the identity of a famous English golfer. If the pub were called the Jug and Jacket,
you'd almost think he owned the place.

St. Cloud promotes itself as an American links, meaning perhaps its shape
owes more to scrapers and bulldozers than Mother Nature and sheep.

A faux Swilcan Bridge.

Belts of rough and mounding separate fairways. Clumps of pampas and cordgrasses are planted within the rough and around bunker edges. In its early years, it has the look of a teenager who's overdone it with flashy makeup and false eyelashes. Time will soften the effect. Square tee boxes show another transatlantic influence. Water is present laterally half the time and as a forced carry on four occasions.

Gators Porch, the first hole when this was still an eighteen-hole track, is a par 5 with a lake at left from the 200- to 100-yard markers. Two, with 150 yards remaining after a 267-yard drive, has a sand hazard at right planted with cordgrass and a kind of garden area. Water runs to the left. A front left bunker guards the square green, which rolls to rear-left and front-left pin positions.

Three is a short one-shot over water to a small promontory upon which sits a deep, forward-flowing green. On four a shelf halfway along the fairway leaves 200 yards to the target. A conspicuous bunker, faced with very tall planks in a railroad-tie effect, lies 50 yards beyond. For this the hole was renamed Wood Face from the original Ridge. Single pot bunkers sit 20 yards off the green entrance and at the rear.

Five doglegs left around a lake. White sand bunkers beacon the correct line. A creek crosses just before the green, which is guarded by two pots at the left.

We cross to the next over a faux Swilcan Bridge, beautifully constructed by one of the members with materials discarded by an Orlando theme park.

The par-3 sixth, King's Saddle, is an upside-down Redan. The green angles right and climbs to the back instead of angling left and sloping to the rear. A front right bunker and two pots well short of the green are the hazards.

Eight requires a 200-yard carry from the tee. A patch of undulating fairway sits to the left as a bailout area. The main feature, in another nod to St. Andrews, is Hell Bunker, 192 yards from the green, more than six feet deep and with enough space to park two cars. The fairway is open beyond. The green gathers to front center.

The bizarre name of the 495-yard ninth, Hookenfächer's Nose, refers to the God of Long Drives, whose head peeks out from the wall behind the tee. I hope the nose is strong enough to withstand titanium. Staggered bunkers lie at both landing areas, and a rear sand hazard guards the angled, kidney-shaped green.

Devil's Pocket begins the next nine with a penal carry over water: 160 yards left is safe; 175 yards right gives the better line in. A cross bunker sits 90 yards out, and a small pond lies behind, hidden from view until one gets close. A

The Devil's Pocket.

tiny greenside bunker is the pocket in question. The wide and shallow putting surface has a center seam and a cant to the rear right quarter.

Young palms form a chute along eleven's 96-yard-long tee box. A greenside bunker is the marker for the target 362 yards distant. Although it looks like a front bunker from afar, it's actually placed at the rear. I really must ask someone about this illusion. From the 150-yard marker the land falls and then rises to the target. A crown at the front of the green sheds to center left and more significantly to rear right.

The thirteenth has two cross bunkers 100 yards from the green in the shape of spectacles, a reference to Carnoustie's fourteenth and the fifth at St. Andrews. This par 5 has a waste area off the tee to the right, which narrows until the 200-yard marker. The two holes rated hardest follow. Parallel par 4s, they are separated by a wide belt of rough. Plans are for bunker additions to tighten up their fairways.

Sixteen is a par 5 dogleg right around a lake. Aiming bunkers sit at the outer apex, 225 yards from the tee. The fairway continues to curl right, with mounding running along the left approach to a flattish green. Two shallow pots sit left at the 100-yard marker. Scottish Revenge finishes this nine.

Narcoossee Road is emerging as a major thoroughfare linking a blossoming area southeast of Orlando International Airport to St. Cloud. The venue is popular with British tourists squeezing in one last round before departure. As fill-in occurs within an ever-expanding boundary, like pieces added to a vast metropolitan jigsaw, golf courses can indicate the probable demographics of their immediate surroundings. The future of Royal St. Cloud looks set to have a silver lining, privately owned but with a municipal outlook.

Falcon's Fire Golf Club

3200 Seralago Boulevard, Kissimmee 34746
(407) 239-5445
www.falconsfire.com

Green fee: $139

Architect: Rees Jones, 1993
Par 72
Blue yardage 6,473; course rating 71.7; slope rating 132
Red yardage 5,417; course rating 71.6; slope rating 126

*Directions: From I-4 exit 65, take 522 (Osceola Parkway) east toward Kissim-
mee 1.8 miles. At Seralago Boulevard turn left; entrance is ahead.*

Ernie Sabayrac is a legend among PGA members. He worked the Houston
Country Club in the 1930s and became the first sales representative of Field and
Flint. Modern-day golfers know their shoes are a joy to wear. Ernie Sabayrac
single-handedly changed the face of the pro shop into a retail outlet. True to
say, some assistants begrudge their role as chocolate bar salespersons; however,
hardened pros know a ringing till is music to the ears of management.

Golf World publishes a list of Top 100 Best Golf Shops, based on sales vol-
ume, sales per square foot, and other criteria. Falcon's Fire has appeared on
the list four times since 1993, and made 2005's All Time Best Golf Shop rating.
From 50,000 rounds in one year, the pro shop sold 300 pairs of shoes, 4,000
hats, 2,000 gloves, 4,200 items of men's clothing, 560 items of ladies' wear, and
56,232 balls (that's 18,744 sleeves of three). The annual turnover of $750,000 in-
cludes casual footwear, glassware, and head covers in the shape of college mascots. Location close to the kingdom of the alliterative rodent means a steady
stream of tourist business to what is essentially a resort course.

The front nine is laid out like the letter B, with holes four and five paired
between the loops. The back nine pairs up four holes, while the rest circle a
large lake. Dramatic fairway and greenside mounding gives elevation to the flat
terrain. Water is a lateral hazard on a third of the holes, and causes a handful

of forced carries from the tee. Bunkers are the chief trouble at Falcon's Fire, 116 of them, unless I misheard starter Wally Moon one misty morning.

Rees Jones placed bunkers to catch the short as well as the long hitter. On the 373-yard first hole, a string of pot bunkers runs for 100 yards on both sides of the landing area. The green is guarded all around. The second fairway kicks right in the final 75 yards, protected by two giant bunkers with grass bullets (see color plate 9). Water lies to the right of the green as an added attraction. The third, a one-shot of 145 yards, plays over water, and sand fronts the target diagonally from the left.

Four needs accuracy off the tee to avoid sand at driving distance on both sides. The small, round green at this 464-yard par 5 tilts right toward a three-bay cape bunker. Five forces a tee shot over wetland and past a stand of tall cypress trees. An open approach plays to an elevated green, which falls forward from a rear-right shelf.

The short sixth has seven bunkers lining the left side from 158 to 280 yards off the tee. The green is tucked away to the right and cornered by pot bunkers. The next, a narrow par 5 with danger around the green, has water and sand to the right and plenty of sand on the left. Names given to holes are clues to built-in traps or hints to how they should be played. Six is indeed Tucked Away, and Lay Up is Rees Jones's steady advice for the seventh.

Number eight is a penal par 3 of 202 yards. Carry the water and avoid bunkers encircling the green. A small bailout area at front left is the best bet for a 187-yard drive. Turning Point brings the round halfway, and after that it's No Turning Back.

The tenth elbows to the right for the second half of its 511 yards. The green is square and guarded at a respectable distance by bunkering. Only two pots and a camera protect the one-shot eleventh, Solitary. Director of Golf Kenny Winn remembers to renew his insurance coverage every year. An ace of 150 yards or longer wins a player $5,000, double on tournament days. Western Golf Properties also offers this incentive on the eighth hole at its other Orlando course, MetroWest. The five aces recorded between the two venues in 2004, Winn declared, were "above average." The odds are one in twenty thousand.

The thirteenth, Bunker Hill, curves around a lake for 382 yards. Fourteen pot bunkers perforate the mounding on the left side of the approach. The fourteenth hole continues around the curve with three bunkers on the left of the landing area. Aim too far right and the approach must clear the lake. A wide bunker waits to the right of the left-sloping green.

There's no letup from here until the eighteenth. Fifteen is a penal carry over water, and the putting surface tilts toward the drink. A ribbon bunker drapes the rear of the green like a scarf. The sixteenth plays over a neck of land with

The home hole and clubhouse.

water at both sides. Water continues on the right, and there's a deep pot beyond the rear of the green. A formidable bunker sits to the left, complete with grass bullet. The penultimate hole is stroke index 2 and curves left around water. The fairway narrows considerably on the approach.

The eighteenth fairway is named Falcon's Fire, a grandstand flourish fronting the Florentine fabric of the clubhouse. This venue has provided a fitting finale to Buick and Oldsmobile National Scrambles and served as a regional qualifying site for the Senior PGA Tour. The National Association of Golf Tournament Directors bestowed on the club their Apex Award in 1999 as one of North America's Top Ten Tournament Facilities. In addition to selling all those hats, Falcon's Fire wears a number itself.

Orange County National Golf Center and Lodge

16301 Phil Ritson Way, Winter Garden 34787
(407) 656-2626
www.ocngolf.com

Green fee: $150

Architects: Phil Ritson, David Harman, and Isao Aoki, 1997

Crooked Cat		Panther Lake
72	Par	72
Green/Red	Tees	Green/Red
6,035/5,236	Yardage	6,298/5,094
69.3/70.3	Course rating	70.7/71.5
121/120	Slope rating	128/125

Directions: From I-4 West exit 64B, take 192 West 6.8 miles to 545 (Avalon Road). Turn right, go 6.8 miles to Phil Ritson Way, turn right again; entrance is 0.4 miles ahead.

From I-4 East exit 55, take 27 North 8.0 miles. At 192 turn right (east) and go 1.5 miles to 545 (Avalon Road). Turn left, go 6.8 miles to Phil Ritson Way, turn right again; entrance is 0.4 miles ahead.

Professional golf creates pressure situations where poise and dignity in execution are required. Multiply this by several thousand intensities, and you have the feeling experienced by competitors at Qualifying School attempting to earn their card for the PGA Tour. Q-School finals take place early in December. Orange County National played host in 2003 and 2005.

In Panther Lake and Crooked Cat, OCN has two championship courses to prove a player's worth—and two tracks in one venue are a logistical fit for any tournament organizer. Both courses have received a four-and-a-half-star rating from *Golf Digest* in recent years. The facility boasts a 42-acre circular driving range, a nine-hole short course, and a 20,000-square-foot practice green. A 46-room lodge enables a concentrated golf experience perfect for group travel.

Attractively priced stay-and-play packages may read like a marketing term but really do make sound economic sense here.

Phil Ritson conceived the idea of OCN, the late David Harman helped in the shaping of it, and Isao Aoki completed the design triumvirate. Ritson's boldness was as admirable as his professional career. Originally from South Africa, he won the Dunlop Masters in 1953 and is recognized as one of America's top teachers. He runs his own institute here at OCN; among his celebrity pupils are K. J. Choi, Billy Mayfair, Isao Aoki, Seve Ballesteros, Ian Woosnam, Curtis Strange, Gary Player, Andre Agassi, and Trini Lopez.

Panther Lake's routing makes it feel the more cohesive of the pair. It is a core course with a loop of three holes (thirteen to fifteen) hanging like a loose stitch of wool from a sweater. Water forces a carry on seven holes, and on six holes it comes into play as a lateral hazard. Live oaks form the majority of vertical features.

Panther's opener stakes a claim to being one of golf's beautiful beginnings. From the elevated tee, the fairway descends over a cross bunker 200 yards away and rises to a square green, which gathers right center. Many of the greens are square. Bunkers tend to be large, free-form, jigsaw-piece shapes. Several re-

"Figures carved into chalk hillsides . . . by early Britons."

Crooked Cat's number seven.

minded me of figures carved into chalk hillsides in southern England by early Britons.

The 170-yard fourth plays over a lake from the back tees or has the water to the left from those forward. The longer carry gives a better angle to the target. Two greenside bunkers prevent use of mounds to the right of the large putting surface. Number six is 40 yards shorter, again over wetland to a square green gathering to the front.

The seventh calls for two carries over wetland. This 536-yard par 5 has a 200-yard strip of fairway for the first landing area; from a forward position it's another 200 yards to the green. A second strip of fairway exists for a three-shot play. Nine's fairway runs parallel to a lake on the right; the green is tucked away behind the water. The eleventh is the most spectacular of the par 3s, a shot over a gully of rough and wetland to a plateau green. The front free-form ribbon bunker is more than adequate distraction.

Fourteen is a monster at 539 yards. Doglegging right, the ground falls away sharply to the left at the first landing area. For the second shot, the fairway narrows to a target with bunkers at front left and rear right. The 162-yard one-shot fifteenth has cordgrass-strewn rough, a lake at left, and attendant bunkers stifling the target. Sixteen's green complex is crowded at the front with another example of this style of elaborate cape bunkering.

Crooked Cat is more open and uncomfortably wears a links tag the way a goat wears a tether. A dearth of trees has the uninformed crying "Links! Links!" when it's really a crafty Crooked Cat. Single trees and small stands are strategically placed hazards rather than fairway linings. Water features on three holes only. An assortment of pots, amoebas, ribbons, and abstract shapes comprise the 72 sand hazards.

The first is quite open, with a row of horizontal sand hazards at the right landing area, not quite the church pew bunkers of Oakmont. On two the player must make a decision on how far downhill to drive. A layup is necessary to negotiate a 100-yard cluster of bunkers preventing all but aerial approach to a two-tier, three-lobed green.

Trees come into play on four. A thick stand narrows the fairway 180 yards out, and a large oak to the left at the 100-yard marker covers a rising chute to an undulating green. The par-4 fifth elbows to the right, its green featuring a pronounced vertical gully in the center and a pot at the rear.

Six is a one-shot play over an intestinally winding bunker. Seven's approach won me over with a jagged Y-shaped bunker running to the hole.

Nine curves left around wetland as a ribbon hazard defines the lower border of the fairway at this side. On the high ground to the right, pot bunkers litter the mounding. The green is tucked away to the left, with a deftly positioned stand of trees blocking direct approach. A heroic cut must pass over water and greenside bunkers; a knockdown draw around the trees is the safer option.

The twelfth curls around wetland to the right, the green tucked away once more, guarded by a solitary pot bunker at greenside left. Sand hazards around the green at the par-3 thirteenth look like Nessie, the Loch Ness monster.

After a stiff dogleg right with an uphill approach at the penultimate hole, the final tee shot plays to an hourglass-shaped fairway. Pot bunkers guard the green, overlooked by faces in the clubhouse window.

Some staff members consider the back nine of Crooked Cat the most difficult, and therefore the most enjoyable; for the recreational golfer, I think Panther Lake wins by a whisker.

A real Tiger played here for the cameras: This is where the "Ham with a Wedge" commercial was filmed. Mr. Woods bounced a golf ball repeatedly off the face of a sand wedge, finally swiping it baseball-style into the outfield.

Highlands Reserve Golf Club

500 Highlands Reserve Boulevard, Davenport 33897
(877) 508-4653
www.highlandsreserve-golf.com

Green fee: $70

Architect: Mike Dasher, 1998
Par 72
Black yardage 6,649; course rating 72.1; slope rating 118
Jade yardage 4,973; course rating 67.4; slope rating 107

Directions: From I-4 exit 55, take 27 North 5.1 miles; entrance is on left.

One book changed my attitude to the grand old game of golf. John Strawn's *Driving the Green* catalogs the building of a residential course in Florida to a design by Arthur Hills. Hills's associate Mike Dasher is a major character in the story, and now a solo operator. When Highlands Reserve general manager Marion Walker hinted at the possibility of meeting the architect, I jumped at the chance.

In an attempt to preserve objectivity, I viewed the course first. The beginning holes are very player-friendly, number one an uphill par 4 to a green with no bunkers. The putting area is 50 yards deep with waves and hollows. Two plays downhill through a wide avenue bordered by pines. Half the holes here have tree barriers; the rest are laid out over naked terrain with large waste areas defined by clumps of cordgrass. One such area lies in the valley 75 yards from the target. The green has a rear right mound and a punchbowl surface.

The third introduces a little difficulty. The fairway passes the waste area shared with the previous hole and climbs steeply to the green. A side bunker contains a solitary mounded tree. I was reminded of a similar hazard behind the eighth green on the Dunes at Seville. The fourth is, like all par 3s here, slightly downhill. The green breaks to the right edge and is guarded by a front pot bunker.

Players have no view of the fifth green until the second shot. The fairway spills over a ridge and downhill, falling away to the left. A small stand of trees

layer-friendly opening.

blocks a right-hand approach to the raised green. The wide putting surface is mounded at rear right and has a vertical gully in the center.

The three closing holes on the front up the ante in difficulty, the last pair being par 5s. Number seven's tee shot must carry 200 yards of waste bunker. A cluster of pot bunkers lie semihidden short and right of the green. The fairway slopes to the right; left is the obvious play, though two greenside pots prevent full use of the contours.

The ninth runs uphill to the left, cascading downhill to the right on approach. A ribbon cape-and-bay bunker off the tee becomes part of a huge waste area taking over the second half of the hole. A handful of pots guard both landing areas. The deep green is false-fronted, and a bunker sits below the right-hand side.

The beauty of the tenth is on the approach. Pine trees border the right while the fairway falls away left into a waste area. The green mirrors this bias, feeding into the front-left quarter. Take an extra club to reach a rear pin position. Eleven has an optical mound only 126 yards from the rear tee box. This is a good line for the target. A bunkered hollow sits below the green on the right; a mound to the left provides a perfect tool to feed the ball to the putting surface.

Dasher's sand hazard on sixteen—is it art?

Holes thirteen through sixteen traverse the side of a hill. The thirteenth offers risk/reward play for varied golfing abilities. A 265-yard drive carries cross bunkers, leaving a 211-yard approach. A landing zone short and left accommodates the shorter hitter. Either way, sand hazards must be crossed 100 yards from the green center. The target is tucked away to the right, on a small shelf, and at a higher elevation than the cross hazards.

"Entrapment" aptly describes the flurry of bunkers covering the landing area on fourteen; anything off the straight and narrow will find the sand. The fairway rises to a plateau green with a pot bunker at front right. This is rated second hardest hole at Highlands Reserve.

Fifteen flows downhill 300 yards off the tee to a large collection bunker. The approach climbs 120 yards past orange trees on the right to an angled, three-tiered green, which flows from rear left. The sixteenth, always rising, doglegs to the right around a large, steep-faced sand hazard. The fairway bunker to the left is the better line off the tee. A long green features a horizontal gully across the center. This is modeled on the Gate (also a sixteenth) at North Berwick, Scotland. The eighteenth brings us home doglegging left through a narrow corridor of pines.

Patiently answering my naïve questions, Mike Dasher explained the pairing of holes to share common rough and irrigation. Given the similarity in terrain, he used his experience on the Dunes at Seville as inspiration for Highlands Reserve. This preempted my question about the bunkered tree on three, and when I thanked him for the easy getaway on one, he was quick to cite influences. "Royal Liverpool is one of my favorite courses. The first hole from the tee looks like nothing. You think, 'What am I doing here?' Then as you progress, the beauty unfolds. I had the same feeling about Palmetto Dunes, South Carolina."

Being a hands-on designer, he visits sites daily, and we made a whirlwind tour of two projects under way in Orlando. Bubbling with ideas for a remodeled par 3 at Orange Lake and rerouting a cart path on a new course, Providence, he puts an enthusiasm into his work that confirms he still has "the best job in the golf business." He talks of his former employer with obvious affection. I asked if he had viewed going solo with any trepidation. With a glint in his eye he admitted he's been perfectly happy since Arthur Hills decided to branch out on his own.

Like just about everybody in the golf industry, Mike Dasher has an interest in something completely different. I got the impression he likes tinkering with machinery—after all, he's "from Georgia Tech and a helluva engineer." If you happen to see a lean figure buzzing around Orlando on an antique German-made motorcycle, it's likely to be Mike dashing between sites, looking into wastelands and routing centerlines.

Southern Dunes Golf and Country Club

2888 Southern Dunes Boulevard, Haines City 33844
(863) 421-4653
www.southerndunes.com

Green fee: $110

Architect: Steve Smyers, 1993
Par 72
Blue yardage 6,803; course rating 72.6; slope rating 129
Red yardage 4,987; course rating 68.8; slope rating 118

*Directions: From I-4 exit 55, go south on 27 for 7.6 miles. At Southern Dunes
Boulevard turn left; entrance is ahead 0.3 miles.*

The freeze of 1989, following those of '83 and '85, destroyed 340 acres of orange groves northwest of Haines City. Citrus growers Terry and Roger Donley wasted little time in finding an alternative use for the land. Project manager Ralph Forrest and architect Steve Smyers determined the course would not be subservient to domestic property in routing or design. Six holes stand on their own, six have homes to one side, and six run through two lanes of housing.

The course sits on a sand ridge twenty-five to forty feet deep, allowing healthy drainage. Seven hundred thousand yards of dirt were moved, though no shaping pans were used, and all mounding and swales are artificial. Pushing up the sugar sand with a small bulldozer created windrows. Imported pines, originally eight to twelve feet in height, and oaks three to five inches in diameter, are now well established, while ornamentals add color and diversity.

Visually Southern Dunes is both buxom and intimidating—huge bunkers in clusters and ribbons, planted with cordgrass; significant elevation changes, especially on the back nine; greens given ample shape and break with a deferent nod to Alister MacKenzie. No two holes are alike, and the variety of shot making required entices players to return time after time.

Opening holes are so important: everybody wants to get a good start, the designer wants to set out his store, and nobody wants a drab double bogey on a rough old nag. The first at Southern Dunes is a steeplechaser. To the right, a ridge with dramatic bunkering looks threatening, also a fairway so undulating it appears the ground is bubbling. Designed to set the nerves aquiver, it gives way to calm after a central pot bunker 140 yards from the tee. From the 150-yard marker a continuous jigsaw cape bunker eats into the left side. The green has a raised spine and falls away to either side, resembling a stingray (minus the tail).

The landing area on the second fairway is a bowl with bunkers on both sides. This time an elaborate bunker runs to the right on the approach. A deep grass hollow lies to the left of the green. Three is a gorgeous par 3, playing downhill to an angled green, guarded right and left and favoring a fade. At a depth of 45 yards, the putting surface falls forward at the front and away at the rear. By the scale of hazards so far, the player realizes that, to corrupt a PGA Tour phrase, "these bunkers are deep." Sand wedges get no rest at Southern Dunes.

Cross bunkers cover the final 100 yards at the par-5 fourth. A bailout chipping area lies beyond them to the right. The conservative approach curls up left of the sand and down to an undulating green with a hump in the center. The fifth features another split fairway decision. The high road to the left allows a better view of the green, while staying right forces a carry over a pond. The greenside drops off deeply behind.

An amphitheater of mounds surrounds the green.

Buxom and intimidating.

The sixth is an attractive one-shot from the back tees, across a large bunker escarpment to the left, downhill to an amphitheater of mounds enclosing the kidney-shaped green. Seven is the hardest hole, a 440-yard dogleg left. Massive cloverleaf bunkers are aiming points across the fairway at the 150-yard mark. A 282-yard tee shot is required to cut the left corner bunkers. The ground rises on the approach, with the fairway pitching left, as does the green, which is guarded on both sides.

A giant bunker off the tee at eight can be cleared with a 210-yard drive. A ribbon cape bunker runs the remaining 185 yards to the right; a similar hazard covers the left edge from 100 yards in. These bunkers narrow the entrance to fourteen paces, and the green tilts forward to receive.

Left is favored off the tee at the ninth, a blind shot uphill over a bunker strewn with clumps of cordgrass and bullets of turf. On this par 5 the fairway dives into a gully at the 200-yard marker. Mounding takes over high ground to the left. Pot bunkers guard front and rear of the raised, angled green.

A long par 4 begins the back nine. The left side looks troublesome but is the better line; a 220-yard drive should be in good position to attack the pin. The fairway is banked on the right, and bunkers occupy ground beyond the 150-

yard mark. The twelfth is a par 5, the green visible 517 yards distant. Shaping left, avoid bunkers off the tee and water that runs all the way to the green. A cluster of pot bunkers tightens the fairway at the first landing area. Thirteen plays uphill, with a bunker off the tee that seems formidable but is not really in play. The fairway drops away sharply to the right on the approach. The unguarded green sheds from the rear left quarter.

At the highest point on Southern Dunes, the 149-yard fourteenth drops over a field of bunkers. The angled green slopes from front right to rear—a downhill Redan hole, let's say, with its front bunker attacked by the Sorcerer's Apprentice. The fifteenth continues downhill to a wide fairway. Cross bunkers cover the right-hand side, the most direct route to the target. From the left the player hits down into the green, which gathers to a lower front shelf.

The next is a par 5 with an open fairway and bunkers at the left of both landing areas. A large optical mound makes blind any approach from the right. The green has a horizontal gully from left center and a pot bunker at front left. According to the mason's original work, the final hole was named Choke Valley, but someone astutely removed the V from the stone tablet by the tee box. After an uphill drive, the approach must clear a cross bunker to a reach the softly undulating green.

Diamondback Golf Club

6501 SR 544 East, Haines City 33844
(863) 421-0437
www.diamondbackgolfclub.net

Green fee: $75

Architect: Joe Lee, 1995
Par 72
Blue yardage 6,410; course rating 71.3; slope rating 132
Red yardage 5,061; course rating 70.3; slope rating 122

*Directions: From I-4 exit 55, go south on 27 for 10.7 miles. At 544 turn left
(east); entrance is on left in 6.0 miles.*

In the early 1990s Grenelefe's three golf courses were so busy that residents
found it hard to get a tee time. A group of thirty-nine partners took steps to
start their own golf club by purchasing 240 acres of wetland across the road.
During a survey, the state botanist found a rare flower and gopher tortoises
among the wildlife. Gopher tortoises share their burrows with diamondback
rattlesnakes; a stuffed example sits in the pro shop. It seemed only natural to
pass over the proposed name, Oak Pines, for something more distinctive.

Joe Lee carved holes through the wetlands, now preservation areas, added
a few lakes, and routed a course where power hitters don't necessarily have an
advantage. This is a thinker's course with emphasis on accuracy off the tee and
at approach. Hurricanes in 2004 carved their own swath through Diamondback to the tune of 1,500 trees.

A par 5 gets the round under way. From an elevated tee, a fairway bunker
lies 240 yards distant. A forced carry over wetland on the second shot leads to
a two-tier, forward-sloping green. Bunkers frame the green entrance on both
sides, and a lone bunker sits rear right. The second tee shot needs to draw
around 225 yards; shorter hitters should fade to open up the hole, leaving a
long-iron approach. The green slopes to front and rear from a center-right
mound.

Plate 1. Hilaman Park: English Parks style.

Plate 2. Windsor Parke: The sixteenth.

Plate 3. Meadowbrook:
The par-3 second.

Plate 4. Ironwood: Magnificent municipal.

Plate 5. LPGA Champions: Grass bullets in bunkers.

Plate 6. Mount Dora: The fifth fairway "as if warped by the sun."

Plate 7. Victoria Hills: Visually stunning.

Plate 8. MetroWest: High society.

Plate 9. Falcon's Fire: Two with a bullet.

Plate 10. Diamondback: A ribbon bunker snakes toward the green.

Plate 11. El Diablo: A hell hole if ever there was one.

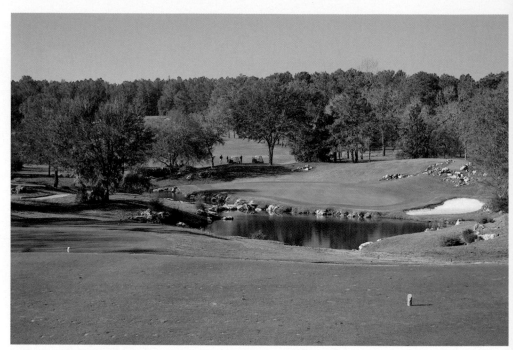

Plate 12. World Woods: Picture perfect—the Rolling Oaks eighth.

Plate 13. Lake Jovita: Elevation changes.

Plate 14. Fox Hollow: 2–iron, 2–iron.

Plate 15. Stoneybrook: Island tee, island green.

Plate 16. Fairwinds: Frightening tee shot on fifteen.

Plate 17. PGA National: A well-covered approach on the Haig.

Plate 18. Okeeheelee: Quiet waters.

Plate 19. Pompano Beach: Welcoming the bump and run.

Plate 20. The Biltmore: The clubhouse and ninth green.

The landscape bordering the third fairway is distinctly swampy. Barbed and tangled trees have a primal look, inducing a feeling of golf at the dawn of time. A wetland cuts access to the green at wedge distance. Beyond, the fairway and green both slope left. Four, a neat 153-yard par 3, plays to a small, coin-shaped target with a bunker to the right (see color plate 10).

The 522-yard fifth angles slightly left at the first landing area. From the 150-yard marker it kicks right. Going for the green in two shots means a carry over water, past a stand of palms, and over rising ground to a well-bunkered green.

From the tee box the seventh appears as though it could dogleg left. More likely this author read too much into the shape of an aiming bunker at the apex of the fairway—the hole actually fades to the right! Three greenside bunkers make aerial approach a necessity. The raised green has a rear-right shelf and spills forward.

Eight has wetland to the left and fairway bunkers at driving distance to the right. The water is named Lake George after one of the founding partners, Dr. George Solomon. The frequency with which his tee shots entered the lake caused one wag to post an eponymous sign. Maybe the good doctor enjoys this

The cloverleaf green triangled by bunkers.

classic view of the course, over the water and rock-lined bank to a green with a pronounced forward slope..

The ninth is a par 4 of 399 yards drifting to the right, with bunkers on either side of the landing area. Aim behind the bunker to the right. Although a blind shot, it is the correct line to the pin. Too far right and the ground drops away or into a greenside bunker. The putting surface has a center left mound from which balls are dispersed. The tenth is rated stroke index 2, a par 5 of 507 yards. Sand hazards are placed at both landing areas to the right; water takes over the left side from the 200-yard marker. A cloverleaf green is triangled by bunkers.

Wetland fronts the tee box at the twelfth. Here I met Bob Pfaff, dressed in waders, on his daily hunt for balls. Holes one, three, thirteen, and fifteen are also favored grounds. He finds on average twenty thousand balls between October and May and, in a dry year, thirty thousand. He calls them his "vodka money" although, being one of the club's founder members, he is far from hard times. In his early eighties, he was long a successful attorney. No mean golfer himself, he qualified on three occasions for the USGA Senior Amateur Championship.

A spectacular trio complete the round. Sixteen doglegs left 496 yards around the lake shared with the eighteenth. Some power hitters have been known to fly balls over the lake, leaving less than 150 yards to the pin. The more sedate player whisks the ball to the first set of bunkers at the angle of the hole. A gentle fairway wood, avoiding bunkers at the second landing area, sends the pill soaring past that of the power hitter. A short iron to six inches from the pin and a tap in secures birdie. The power hitter's approach lands at the rear of the green and he three-putts for par. Tortoise beats hare once again, although imagination exceeds ability in my case.

Seventeen needs enough club to carry the greenside bunker on this 177-yard, one-shot hole. A beautiful dogleg right finishes the round. A 225-yard tee shot to the left-hand side of the fairway is ideal. The lake and a continuous beach bunker line one side of the approach to the receptive green with one bunker at the rear.

In the clubhouse roll of honor, Dr. George Solomon is listed as having scored a hole-in-one on three of Diamondback's par 3s. Should he ever ace the thirteenth hole, the Solomon Slam would be worthy of more than a set of steak knives. Perhaps he could take home the Lake George sign.

Lekarica Hills Golf Club

1650 Highland Park Drive, Lake Wales 33898
(863) 679-9478
www.lekarica.com

Green fee: $35

Architects: Wayne Stiles and John Van Kleek, 1927
Par 72
Green yardage 6,116; course rating 69.3; slope rating 124
Silver yardage 5,174; course rating 69.1; slope rating 113

Directions: From 60 in Lake Wales, take 17 South (Scenic Highway) 2.3 miles. At Village of Highland Park, turn left and go 0.2 miles to Highland Park Drive. Turn left; entrance is on left in 0.5 miles.

The course formerly known as Highland Park Hills is one of the oldest in Florida. The Village of Highland Park was a planned upscale community begun in the mid-twenties, when Lake Wales was in its prime. Publisher and author Edward Bok had gardens to the north designed by Frederick Law Olmsted, famous for planning Central Park in New York. Olmsted also designed the exclusive Mountain Lake Estates nearby. Highland Park was meant as a compatible local addition. Railroad magnate I. A. Yarnell built La Casa De Josephina, a huge Moorish castle, on the property for his wife. Wayne Stiles and John Van Kleek, a New England–based team, with Walter Hagen on their books as a consultant, planned the course, which opened just in time for the Great Depression to stifle growth in the community.

Decades of maintenance without significant improvement left it stagnant and potential fodder for bulldozers. Topography was on its side: a sandy ridge gives elevation changes of 110 feet to the layout. Saved by a Pennsylvania potato farmer, Bob Weaver, the course has been undergoing improvements. An out-of-the-way gem, he renamed it for his children: Lesley, Kara, and Eric.

Though it is short in length, walkers may get more than they bargained for on this cardiac course. None of the par 5s measures more than 500 yards, but half the track plays on a steep spur of hillside. I'm sure some players will feel as

View from behind the fifth green.

though they're on maneuvers. Greens are in excellent condition. Sheer-sided bunkers look like pond excavations before lining and filling.

Commencing with two bunkers to the left at driving distance, a small crown green waits with hazards at front left and rear. The second tee shot is to the angle of the dogleg, through a small opening and over water, which then runs the length of the hole to the right. The raised green tilts left, and a bunker guards the entrance at front right.

The third is a one-shot of 155 yards. The green, average-sized at 4,500 square feet, feeds to the right. Four doglegs left, hitting down into the landing area from the tee. A bunker lies to the right. Staggered bunkers line the approach, and a hazard takes greenside left. The putting surface slopes gently forward in the front half.

Five plays longer than its 360 yards, since it climbs steeply from 125 yards out. A deep cross bunker sits at the center 50 yards from the plateau green. The sixth bowls along downhill 352 yards. The 150-yard marker is the best line, as two bunkers cover the left-side approach. A bunker at front left guards the elevated green.

Nearest-the-pin always quickens the pulse on golf society days; number seven is my candidate of the four par 3s at Lekarica. Sand hazards triangle the target, and the tee lines up with one on the right. Measuring 3,000 square feet, the green slopes into the center from the rear left quarter; the right half of the putting surface slopes to the right edge.

Number eight doglegs right 322 yards. A barrier of tall pines stands at the inner angle for those power players attempting to cut the corner. Even if they succeed, a big bunker greenside waits for anything short. The elevated green is biased from the back right quarter. The ninth plays 490 yards with bunkers at both sides of the first landing area. The ground rises sharply from the 200-yard marker.

The turn is away from the clubhouse. Ten is a downhill par 3, the green lobed by two front bunkers and a drop-off at the rear.

Eleven runs just shy of 400 yards in length, and the first shot vaults uphill going left. A bunker sits 250 yards off the tee. The land dips on approach and rises to a rear-sloping platform green.

The twelfth continues the uphill-dogleg-left trend, but is shorter by 40 yards. A sand hazard guards the angle on a blind brow of the hill. From here, the remaining 150 yards climb gradually to a plateau green, raised at the rear and guarded by a front left bunker.

The seventeenth.

At the highest point of the property, thirteen runs alongside a citrus grower's processing plant. The five holes on this ridge were surrendered to orange production during World War II. A waste area lies left off the tee. These "native" areas at Lekarica may be authentic, although they have the appearance of green turf stripped away for cosmetic effect.

Fourteen rolls downhill in par-5 mode. Palm trees block an approach from the right at 90 yards. A pot bunker sits at front left. A sand hazard as big as the green waits to the right of the punchbowl putting surface.

The last four head back to the clubhouse on more level ground. Fifteen and sixteen are par 4s of similar length. The first fairway is straight and hides a bunker 20 yards off the target to the right. The next angles right from the 150-yard mark; a deep bunker rims the left side of the green.

Bamboo stands frame the left of the seventeenth, a 160-yard one-shot. The alignment on the tee box is askew; watch also for the horizontal gully and line of cordgrass before the green. The putting surface gathers to the right edge, with slight breaks front and rear.

Eighteen, a par 5 of 469 yards, elbows right. Bunkers lie left 250 yards off the tee, 125 yards from the green, and greenside. The baizelike surface breaks to the front right quarter.

Highland Park Hills was close to obscurity, nestling in a sleepy backwater, and who knows what might have happened if a new course had opened nearby and gobbled up golfers. A historical oddity being upgraded into a working charm from the profits of Pennsylvania potatoes; when catering at Lekarica gets sorted out, I'll expect bangers and mash on the menu.

Part III

Tampa Area
and Gulf Coast

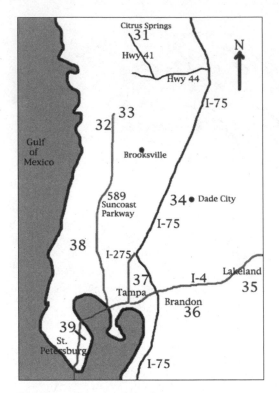

Tampa to Lakeland and North

31 El Diablo
32 The Dunes
33 World Woods
34 Lake Jovita
35 Cleveland Heights
36 Bloomingdale
37 The Claw at USF
38 Fox Hollow
39 Mangrove Bay

El Diablo Golf and Country Club

10405 N Sherman Drive, Citrus Springs 34434
(352) 465-0986
www.eldiablogolf.com

Green fee: $55

Architect: Jim Fazio, 1998
Par 72
Blue yardage 6,232; course rating 71.7; slope rating 130
Red yardage 5,144; course rating 69.8; slope rating 117

Directions: El Diablo is off 41 west of Ocala, 3 miles south of Dunellon.

*From I-75 North exit 329, take 44 west 15.0 miles to Inverness. At 44 West
[45], turn right, go 1.0 miles to 41 North, and turn right again. In 14.4 miles, at
Citrus Springs Boulevard, make another right. Go 0.3 miles to Athenia Drive
and turn right; entrance is on right.*

*From I-75 South exit 352, take 40 west for 17.5 miles. At 41 South turn left,
go 7.4 miles to Citrus Springs Boulevard, and turn left again. Go 0.3 miles to
Athenia Drive and turn right; entrance is on right.*

In the middle of nowhere but soon to be somewhere, Citrus Springs has extensive plans for housing lots—that is, lots of housing. Another golf club already
exists at Citrus Springs, but the development plans around El Diablo appear
less crowded. It's enough to make me wish I'd got in on the ground floor. Reality
is, I'll just have to make do with family-permitted visits.

This is a woodland course defined by pines and oaks and marked changes
in elevation. The greens are so lush they look painted—a characteristic of Flo-
raDwarf, a hybrid turf developed at the University of Florida. When the Bahia
rough lies dormant in winter, its brown edging enhances the greenness of overseeded fairways. Pansies planted around the live oaks are a decorative touch.
Squirrels abound. Apart from their chattering, you will hear little else.

For the golf, this is the reply of Jim Fazio to brother Tom's work down the
road at World Woods. It could be said El Diablo is the result of the architect's
own meeting at the crossroads. This is among his best work. Not a stinger in

From the second tee, three sand craters sit fairway right.

terms of length, it is deemed difficult enough to host qualifying rounds for the U.S. Open, Florida's Senior Four Balls Championship, and the NCAA Division 1 intercollegiate two-day event in March. This venue regularly receives Best Place to Play awards.

The tests of greatness are the two outward and two home holes, although I found other candidates in the round. From the second tee, three sand craters sit fairway right. Clear them and keep to the right along this 526-yard par 5; waste and pot bunkers cover the left. The green pitches forward, with a center left depression.

El Diablo's par 3s are holes three, six, thirteen, and fifteen, decreasing in distance as the round progresses. Three has a pot bunker in front catching those that have underclubbed. To the left, a large bunker proves a real draw. Six is the simplest: 154 yards with trees narrowing the opening to a forward-tilting green. Thirteen has a tree blocking the left side, forcing many a push right, where a greenside bunker collects. Fifteen is only 134 yards and plays a little downhill. The green slopes from rear left to front right. The main hazard is a front pot bunker seven feet in depth—a little deeper by the time I extricated my ball. A hell hole if ever there was one (see color plate 11).

The fourth fairway splits from the 150-yard marker. The higher, left side runs straight to the green; lower right means a carry over a linear waste area strewn with rocks and planted with cordgrass.

From a blind ridge at driving distance on the fifth, the land rolls down to deep scrub to the right. The 368-yard seventh is also blind off the tee, breaking rapidly downhill as the ball disappears. Choose a club to get within 150 to 100 yards of the flag. From here on, bunkers occupy the higher ground as the fairway tumbles to the right. Large grass hollows trap anything too long or wide.

Nine is an uphill dogleg left and rated hardest hole, though the fairway is generous at the 150-yard marker. A steep bank forms a wall to the right of the green. Resist the temptation to bounce your approach off the wall: a grass hollow below will snaffle such attempts.

The difficulty ratings of ten and eleven bemuse me. The tenth, stroke index 4, is a straight 408-yard par 4 with staggered fairway bunkers. The green is deep and narrow and falls away at the rear. Number eleven, stroke index 12, is considerably more testing. After a forced carry over an ornamental lake, the fairway undulates uphill all the way. The plateau green lies behind two deep, steep-faced bunkers. Admittedly eleven is 50 yards shorter than ten, but the rise in elevation and large obstacles more than compensate.

Twelve is high on the gorgeous index. A par 5 with a blind tee shot, the ever-so-wide fairway spills down to where trouble begins at the 150-yard marker. A waste bunker runs to the right, and trees frame the target on three sides. A high, soft fade should neatly avoid the verticals and bunkers hugging the rear of the green.

With wonderful economy, the next three holes share the same parcel of land: the length of the two par 3s combined equals the fourteenth. Aim at the bunker cluster to the left and cut a shot to the widest point of the fairway. A greenside nest of bunkers necessitates aerial approach to the warped putting surface.

Sixteen's 341 yards play through a tight avenue of trees to a lean fairway. The two tier green slopes to the front right quarter. A waste area, with a Zen-like rock sitting meditatively in the middle, must be carried from the seventeenth tee. Oaks line the left, pines the right of the hole. Bunkers surround the flat green.

Though named Hallelujah! the eighteenth has been more dramatically baptised by *Golf Digest* as Hell's Half Acre, with a complimentary wink to Pine Valley. The final 125 yards of ribbon fairway pass stony ground on the right. When leaving the green, don't look back. The trees are hung with Spanish moss of an eeriness conjuring visions of voodoo.

The Dunes Golfers Club

18200 Seville Clubhouse Drive, Brooksville 34614
(352) 596-7888

Green fee: $45

Architect: Arthur Hills, 1986
Par 72
Blue yardage 6,653; course rating 72.1; slope rating 130
Red yardage 5,236; course rating 70.8 Slope rating 118

*Directions: From the northern end of 589 (Suncoast Parkway) turn left (west)
on 98 (Ponce De Leon Boulevard) and go 4.4 miles. At 98 [55] (Commercial
Way) turn left (south) and go 3.4 miles; entrance is on left.*

Hernando County in recent years was the fastest growing county in Florida.
Previously, for golfers, Hernando was something of a drive-through between
Ocala and Tampa. But with World Woods, Hernando Oaks, and Pete Dye's
recent Southern Hills, this has the makings of a golf destination as lauded as
Long Island or the Monterey Peninsula. The Dunes at Seville banged the drum
twenty years ago, way ahead of its time in Hernando.

The Dunes is two miles west of a younger rival and two miles closer to the
ocean. It has been the voice in the wilderness since 1986 calling owners, designers, and players to the region. At 110 feet above sea level, the terrain is rugged,
providing significant changes in elevation. The lay of the land favors large waste
areas, so prevalent nowadays. With little water on the course, the main hazard
at the Dunes is sand. A dozen bunkers are on the massive side, some have
trees growing within, but strictly speaking they are bunkers. Trees line most
fairways, though the course does not have to rely on them for its beauty.

The boom in development is affecting Seville, once an isolated golf course
with a few homes. New owners have plans for an access road close to the northern end of the Suncoast Parkway. This isn't the only golf course development
where building lots have remained in a virgin state for over ten years. Increasing
numbers of baby boomers are now reaching retirement age. "Another winter
shut indoors in the Frozen North, dear, or shall we try Florida?" Build-it-and-

Number eight's bunker tree.

they-will-come is the impression I received from the local people. Jim Crocci, the head golf professional, is looking forward to his new role as property developer. He expects the Dunes to turn private eventually. Prospective residents, and the rest of us, now have incentive enough to visit as soon as possible.

A wonderful thing it is to play across a valley. The sweep of fairway reeling down the hill like green silk and hoisted to the other side by a tiny-looking bobbin five hundred yards away. Best to unravel this hole from the right-hand side; too long or left and sand swallows the ball. Hole two doglegs left with a bunker at the angle. The green is guarded by a bunker at front left. The third doglegs right. Strong players can cut the corner, flirting with trees and a sand hazard.

Please excuse me for recording a rare success in print, but I made par on the 392-yard fourth. I duck-hooked my approach into trees 60 yards short of the green. A gentle pitch with a 9-iron found the raised, flat green, and I rolled a twelve-foot putt into the cup. Honestly, Reader, the infrequency of such moments in my golf history is enough to make them noteworthy.

Jim Crocci joined us on the next tee. I went to pieces. Found the trees. Snowman. Ruined the card. The fifth is a 537-yard par 5 with a wide landing

The par-3 thirteenth.

area but on rising ground. The approach tunnel narrows, and a front left bunker is all the protection this green needs—especially as your correspondent hooked wide of the bunker with his fourth shot. Fluffed. Chipped on, lagged up, and accepted the gimme from Jim. "Been playing long?" he asked. I winced as, with wonderful timing, our playing partner's cell phone bleeped something by Beethoven.

On the 144-yard sixth, my tee shot found the cape between a pair of deep bunkers beside the green. Lying below my feet, legs and clubface wide open, I swung across the ball. Rising up in the air with all the elegance of a startled grouse, it plopped onto the green and waddled away from the pin. After overcooking the first putt by eight feet, I slipped a downhill left-to-right slider into the hole to save bogey. Enough of my expertise, it's your turn.

Eight is a beautiful 187-yard one-shot challenge. A draw is favored here, as the target lies uphill. Short and left will find deep bunkers; a mammoth bunker with an island tree sits behind the green catching anything too strong. The ninth has a waste area to the left, while the curving fairway falls away to the right and trouble in the trees. Clubbing up is the key to approaching this raised, split-level green.

The tenth is a short par 4 with fairway tilted to the right. The green sits on a small shelf ringed by a gully to the lower, right-hand side. Two pots guard the left. Eleven features a bunker cut diagonally across the fairway to the 150-yard marker. The small green is hipped by mounds, and a pond lies off to the right.

Twelve plays to a broad, gently undulating fairway, which rises significantly to a plateau. A large pot bunker dominates the center of the landing area. A wrap-around bunker frames all but the entrance to the left-sloping green.

Although short at 131 yards, the thirteenth has a small, coin-shaped green tilting left. The land falls away quickly to the left, front and rear. The par-3 sixteenth requires the same pinpoint accuracy as thirteen, but from 50 yards farther.

Back-to-back par 5s test the weary hacker at the end, but capable golfers will relish the prospect of a birdie-birdie finish. Both play uphill. The seventeenth fairway has a waste area to be crossed at driving distance. The second shot is blind; beware a greenside bunker at front left. The home fairway tilts left, with the final objective a plateau green surrounded by sand. My approach sailed happily over both toward the car park.

Now and then I am reminded I have something in common with Mark O'Meara, Nick Faldo, Bernhard Langer, and Seve Ballesteros—we were all born in the same year. Did they peak too soon?

World Woods Golf Club

17590 Ponce De Leon Boulevard, Brooksville 34614
(352) 796-5500
www.worldwoods.com

Architect: Tom Fazio, 1993

Pine Barrens		Rolling Oaks
$130	Green fee	$120
	(both courses same day: $180)	
71	Par	72
Back/Forward	Tees	Back/Forward
6,458/5,301	Yardage	6,520/5,245
71.4/71.0	Course rating	71.6/70.1
123/124	Slope rating	130/123

Directions: From I-75 exit 301, take 50 west for 10.6 miles to Brooksville. At US 41 North [98] turn right. In 0.8 miles, bear left on 98 North [700] (Ponce De Leon Boulevard) and go 10.1 miles; entrance is on right.

From 589 (Suncoast Parkway) exit right on 98 [700] (Ponce De Leon Boulevard) and go 0.8 miles; entrance is on left.

When World Woods opened in 1993, the venue was immediately installed on lists of top places to play by leading golf publications. Pine Barrens was rated Best New Course to Play, with Rolling Oaks in eighth position. In the Best Daily Fee Course in the U.S.A. category, Pine Barrens wins so often that it almost owns the title. Rolling Oaks is never far behind but in a sense is the younger fraternal twin. Pine Barrens has a brace of holes, fourteen and fifteen, ranked among the top 500 golf holes in the world.

Is World Woods the best work of Tom Fazio? Try choosing a best Beatles song or best Van Gogh painting. If anything, World Woods is his White Album with a bonus CD of studio fragments and outtakes. To paraphrase his sleeve notes, he contemplated the land available in the way a sculptor allows a block of marble to suggest the figure within.

Pine Barrens is of unquestionable beauty and woven gracefully around a 44-acre waste area of sand. Grounding a club is permitted, but the ball must be played as it lies; there's no relief for a plugged ball. Tall pine trees line most fairways. In such a picture-book setting, the score almost becomes an after-thought.

The first fairway rolls comfortably downhill to a crown green. On two the waste area kicks in, the fairway slopes right, and the unprotected green drops to the front left. Number three is a one-shot of 146 yards; it and the fifteenth are the only holes where water comes into play. The fourth is a truly monumental hole, engulfed by a vast expanse of waste area. On this par 5 of 480 yards, the golfer is always climbing to a plateau green. The sandy waste area in front is deadly. Landing a ball on the green is like hitting onto the roof of a house. The 7,200-square-foot putting surface breaks from a crown in the center.

Five's fairway slims to a 12-yard width over the final 100 yards. The cornflake green is watched over by a formidable pot bunker. After the tee shot at six, the waste area features again noticeably on the back nine. Holes eight and nine have their own regional waste area. The eighth is a blind tee shot; left is the widest part of the fairway. The ninth green is pinched at both sides, waste lying to the left and a big pot bunker balking the right.

On twelve the fairway dips into a hollow with 250 yards to go. Looking to the end of the fairway, no flagstick is visible. You'll find it perched away to the right on a high table, on one of the smaller greens, guarded by sand and trees.

The fourteenth outdoes the fourth in length, again always rising. A conventional bunker to the left had me thinking I'd reached the green, only to discover another 100 yards remaining.

Pine Barrens number twelve.

Fifteen is a wee par 4 of 313 yards. A split fairway provides classic risk-and-reward opportunity. Decide on a 213-yard carry over water to the right fairway, or on a conservative placement to the left. The green sits in a tiny bowl on the extreme right, the lowest point of this hole.

The sixteenth is an awesome 205-yard par 3 with waste area running from tee to green and steeply banked at the right-hand side. Eighteen has a forgiving landing area for the tee shot and doglegs left, undulating all the way to the finish.

Rolling Oaks shares some terrain with its sister track. Holes one to three, and nine and ten, have similar sandy structure and drainage, but generally this eighteen is more lush and densely wooded. Bunkering is conventional. Course superintendent Brad Barbee summed it up: "We mow our rough, Barrens have to rake theirs." Cory Bell, superintendent of Pine Barrens, admits there is a healthy, jocular rivalry between the pair. Director of grounds Jimbo Rawlings ensures any competition is of mutual benefit.

Oaks's third tee shot is played into a field of sand quilts. Having negotiated this par 5, look back up the fairway: all the sand has disappeared. The fifth is also a par 5 in the most open quarter of the property. I felt strangely exposed and vulnerable after hours spent in the enchanted woods.

Number eight is a classic golfing landscape. From an elevated tee, the shot is 148 yards over a rock-lined pond with a bunker to the right (see color plate 12).

Rolling Oaks breaks and tumbles toward the thirteenth hole, a par 3 of 186 yards, hemmed in by rocks and a pot bunker at the right. Thereafter the course climbs steadily to the end. Sixteen is a one-shot hole of dramatic elevation. The final fairway elbows down to a lake at the right, then climbs to a flag guarded by pot bunkers on both sides.

Many visitors play both courses the same day. Strong players will find this a joy, others a workout. My advice for the recreational golfer is to spend two days here. Take advantage of the 22-acre driving range, the par-3 course, and three practice holes—a par 5, a par 4, and a par 3. One could devote an entire day to the practice facilities. On first seeing the two acres of putting course, presented as though by a sommelier displaying a label, I started laughing. I left World Woods with tears in my eyes.

A sign above the door of head golf professional Scott Wyckoff's office reads: "Our primary goal is to provide the greatest experience guests ever encountered at a golf facility." This goal is achieved daily. If golf isn't as good as this in the afterlife, there are going to be many disappointed souls.

Lake Jovita Golf and Country Club— South Course

12900 Lake Jovita Boulevard, Dade City 33525
(352) 588-9200
www.lakejovita.com

Green fee: $119

Architects: Kurt Sandness and Tom Lehman, 1999
Par 72
Blue yardage 6,690; course rating 72.2; slope rating 133
Red yardage 5,145; course rating 70.3; slope rating 121

Directions: From I-75 exit 285, take 52 east 5.3 miles; entrance is on left.

From Dade City, at the junction of 52 and 301, take 52 west 4.5 miles; entrance is on right.

"Rolling hills, ancient hardwood forests and natural lakes" reads the flyer extolling a gated community with grand housing and expensive cars. Lake Jovita exudes an air of luxury and affluence—so much so that it will likely turn private. I hope stay-and-play villa packages will still be an option, because if you want bang for your buck, golf is more economical here than in either Miami Beach or Key West. *Golf Digest* rated the South Course the eleventh-best golf course in Florida and one of the Top 10 New Upscale Courses in the United States in 2000. Tom Lehman said one attraction of the site was the trees: "The day this course opened, it looked like it had been here for decades!"

Heavily bunkered with some 120 sand hazards in all, the course has no unprotected greenside. Wetland and water force seven carries; five holes are dry. Scorecard diagrams of green shapes resemble an amoeba trying to punch its way out of a paper bag. The putting surfaces are among the largest in Florida. The few I measured average more than 8,000 square feet. All have enough breaks and cupping areas to meet the needs of a major championship.

Two PGA Tour-winning professionals live at Lake Jovita, so it is not surprising to find pyramids of clean, shiny practice balls at the driving range. This

The eleventh, a 94-foot drop from tee to green.

place was more upscale than I'd imagined and with an opening as scenic as any Constable painting (see color plate 13). From high elevation the fairway drops dramatically and tilts right to stepped landing areas 200–250 yards off the tee. Trees frame both sides. The approach must thread through a narrow opening and over wetland up to a green protected by two bunkers at front right and a pot at center left. The 10,000-square-foot putting surface flows from a raised quarter at rear left.

The 531-yard second has a penal carry of 180 yards over wetland to staggered bunkers at the landing area. A whopping 275-yard drive should clear all trouble. There's plenty of room for a layup between the 150- and 100-yard markers. A pond precludes ground approach from 90 yards. A sliver of fairway runs left to the target. The giant forward-sloping green dwarfs bunkers front and rear.

A heroic carry is called for at the third, where a lake fronts the tee and borders the hole to the left. A cross bunker in the center of the fairway must be cleared to set up ideal approach position. Bunkers from 75 yards out surround the green, which has a central ridge at the rear.

The penal 181-yard carry over water at the fourth had me wondering if this intensity could be maintained. An alternative set of tees has the water to the left, but overhanging oaks inhibit the right-hand side of this par 3. Interesting breaks in the green include rear right quarter to center, center back to left, and a forward slope in the front half.

The fifth, measuring a shade less than 400 yards, is a blissful escape from heroic necessity. A bunker cluster sits halfway along the fairway to the right, and oaks cover the left from 120 yards out. The green, bunkered on both sides, slopes forward and to rear right from a central ridge. It seems mundane compared to what's gone before.

Six is a 425-yard dogleg left and is rated hardest hole. A forgiving landing area at the apex leaves 180 yards uphill through an ever-narrowing chute. Bunkers guard both front quarters, and the green spills forward in three steps. The one-shot seventh would be a breather if it weren't for the wetland to the left and two front bunkers in a row.

Approach at the 501-yard ninth is the key to the hole. The green is tucked away to the right and surrounded by bunkers. A lake lies to the right, and oak trees block access from the second landing area. A cross bunker occupies the center of the fairway 80 yards from the green.

I had chosen Lake Jovita assuming the routing was part of an old course built by Wayne Stiles and John Van Kleek in the 1920s. Its history is recorded on a commemorative plaque by the eleventh tee. The earlier development fell foul of the Great Depression; sadly, the old course no longer exists.

Eleven drops 94 feet over 537 yards from tee to green. From a blind tee shot, bunkers sit to the right of the first landing area. The second shot is also blind, playing down a series of shelves into a narrowing fairway around the 150-yard marker. Two bunkers lie left 130 yards from the green and another right 50 yards off the front. A lake rings the rear.

Hazards are difficult to avoid at the 539-yard thirteenth, basically a field of seventeen bunkers. Staggered clusters at driving distance precede a stretch of wetland 220 yards from the green. Bunkers cover both sides of the approach. The angled green slopes to the front and rear right from a central ridge.

Sixteen requires a 200-yard carry over wetland to reach the fairway, but only 160 yards from the white tees. Rising toward the green, the ground falls away to the right at the 100-yard marker with a trio of bunkers saving a foray into a thick tree barrier.

Seventeen is an uphill right-hand slider with a steady progression of bunkers at both sides. Left of center is favored for the tee shot, as mounding to the right blocks view of the green. The two-tier putting surface drops from rear right to front left. The 400-yard home hole plays downhill to a well-protected landing zone. The fairway curls left to an equally well-bunkered green.

Kurt Sandness completed a second track at Lake Jovita. The North Course opened in 2005 and appears, at first inspection, more open, a little bit longer, and just as tough as sister South.

- - - - - - - - - - - -

Cleveland Heights

2900 Buckingham Avenue, Lakeland 33803
(863) 682-3277
www.lakelandgov.net/chgolf/home.html

Green fee: $30 (7–11 a.m. tee times include lunch)

Architects: William Flynn and Howard Toomey, 1925

Blue/Red	A+C	B+A	C+B
Par	72/73	72/74	72/73
Yardage	6,517/5,551	6,345/5,374	6,426/5,445
Course rating	70.9/71.5	70.0/71.0	70.3/71.1
Slope rating	123/120	122/121	123/120

Directions: From I-4 exit 32, take 37 (Florida Avenue) south 5.4 miles. At Edgewood Drive turn left, go 0.7 miles to Buckingham Avenue, and turn right; entrance is on left.

From 60, take 37 (Florida Avenue) north 8.3 miles. At Edgewood Drive turn right, go 0.7 miles to Buckingham Avenue, and turn right; entrance is on left.

Cleveland Heights is unofficial home to the Futures Tour, the LPGA up-and-coming division. Mingling with the rising stars are some experienced players who wish to remain competitive and retain their LPGA Tour cards. These seasoned competitors' know-how must be a benefit to the youngsters. The Futures season opens at Cleveland Heights in March. December brings Qualifying School to Lakeland with an international field of more than three hundred female competitors contending over three courses. The hotly contested final round returns to Cleveland Heights.

The three nines are evenly balanced. Course C has two tough holes in the middle, B has the hardest finish, and A's fifth hole is a candidate for hardest hole of all. Fairways are wide open, with only a handful of forced carries over water. The difficulty factor comes in when the player's short game is tested—bunkers are strategically placed around raised greens with drop-offs at the rear.

Course A opens with a straight par 4 downhill. A dry creek bed runs across the fairway 70 yards from the green. Cross the creek over a wee stone bridge, a recurrent rustic note. A 202-yard par 3 follows, as players hit into a big target with a lower right shelf. A bunker off to the right is not really in play. Three and four are straight par 4s of medium difficulty. On leaving the third green, check the pin placement on five, which is a 440-yard dogleg around a lake to the right. Keep left off the fifth tee. Accuracy is demanded on the approach, for two bunkers lie left of the green. To the right, the greenside collar spills into the lake. For a high handicapper, bogey is a respectable score here.

The par-5 sixth narrows off the tee, the left side being favored for the second shot. With 100 yards remaining, the fairway kicks right to an elevated, kidney-shaped green hipped by bunkers. Seven's green is tucked away to the left and more extreme than the sixth. The raised green complex, with bunkers biting into the entrance, resembles a key lime pie with three giant scoops missing.

Eight is a par 5 with a blind tee shot over a ridge. The landing area has plenty of room, but again play favors the left side. A front bunker forces aerial entry, and the putting surface slopes to the front left quarter. The ninth is the hardest par 3 at the Heights, uphill to a small target with hazards front and right. The green slopes away from the rear center.

The Heights clubhouse occupies the highest point at the facility, so Course B begins with two downhill holes. The third doglegs left, requiring a 175-yard

Straight par 4 downhill.

Key lime pie with giant scoops missing.

carry over a creek. From here it's a straight shot to a forward-sloping, left-bunkered green. Planted by the sixth tee, a jacaranda tree is dedicated "to all women who have walked this way." The seventh's main hazard is water, at both sides off the tee and continuing all the way on the right. The target is elevated, with large bunkers on either side, and tilts from the rear right quarter.

Given its 464-yard length, number eight is better treated as a three-shot by high handicappers. Pines and oaks form the left-hand side, with water on the right. The green is tucked away on the left and bunkered. Number nine angles left across a dry creek and then uphill to a small green with heavy undulation.

Course C starts favoring a left-to-right shape. The third, a par 4 of 348 yards, gives an easy option for most. Drives longer than 220 yards will reach water running across the fairway; a 282-yard carry will stay dry. The green has pot bunkers on both sides and slopes to the front. There's another forced carry at number four, 157 yards over a creek. The hole elbows left, and water runs to the right of the approach.

A jumbo carry over water is needed at the par-5 fifth, where aiming left will more likely find land than going for glory. The day I visited, so many groups had used the alternative tees that a flock of skimmers were squatting comfortably on the blue tee box. The second shot plays along an avenue lined by pines to a raised, flat green with one greenside bunker at left. The one-shot eighth, at only 168 yards, is trickier than length and rating suggest. The green has bunkers at every corner, and overshooting to the right will find a pond.

The Cleveland connection comes from H. A. Stahl, a development tycoon from Ohio. He was visiting the Cleveland Indians during their spring training in Lakeland when the local chamber of commerce offered him the opportunity to emulate the success of John D. Rockefeller's Cleveland Heights in the North. Stahl purchased 540 acres by Lake Hollingsworth; his golf course opened in 1925 and was one of the prime Florida golf destinations of its day. The Great Depression found the Heights being sold to the city, which has operated it ever since.

The original eighteen-hole course's routing was altered and locally based Ron Garl added a third nine in the 1980s. Across the road on Buckingham Avenue, where there are now tennis courts and a children's playground, the course started and finished by Lake Hollingsworth. Today's exclusive Lakeland Yacht and Country Club was once the old clubhouse.

The 1940s added further cachet to Lakeland with Frank Lloyd Wright's campus buildings for South Florida College. This is an opportunity to see the largest collection of his buildings in one place. I wondered why Cleveland Heights has no fancy names for its nines—the Lake, the Land, the Heights, for example. But after gazing at the form-follows-function style of Wright's work, I think he would appreciate the simplicity of its nomenclature. For Lakeland students and Futures Tour hopefuls, it's as simple as ABC.

Bloomingdale Golfers Club

4113 Great Golfers Place, Valrico 33594
(813) 655-4105
www.bloomingdalegolf.com

Green fee: $79

Architect: Ron Garl, 1983
Par 72 (blue), 73 (red)
Blue yardage 6,651; course rating 71.8; slope rating 123
Red yardage 5,397; course rating 72.1; slope rating 132

Directions: From I-75 exit 254, take 301 south 0.7 miles to Bloomingdale Avenue and turn left (east). In 4.2 miles, at Bell Shoals Road, turn right. Go 1.2 miles to Glenhaven Drive, turn left, go 0.3 miles to Nature's Way Boulevard, and turn right. In 0.3 miles, entrance is on left (Great Golfers Place.)

From 60 (Brandon Boulevard) take Lithia Pinecrest Road 3.8 miles. At Bloomingdale Avenue turn right (west), go 1.5 miles to Bell Shoals Road and turn left. Go 1.2 miles to Glenhaven Drive, turn left, go 0.3 miles to Nature's Way Boulevard, and turn right. In 0.3 miles, entrance is on left (Great Golfers Place.)

In its early years Bloomingdale boasted two hundred members with single-digit handicaps, seventy-three of whom had handicaps of three or less. Nervous and hopeful professionals sweated their way through PGA Tour qualifying rounds here, among them Lee Janzen. It is a credit to the design team that Bloomingdale was rated Tampa Bay's number-one course nine years in a row.

The clubhouse atmosphere is Old World reserve, dark wood furnishings, and armchairs in the locker rooms. Books on golf architecture and design sit on the lobby coffee table. Lining the walls are black-and-white photos of mid-twentieth-century golf heroes: Ben Hogan, Byron Nelson, Jimmy Demaret, Hogan, Hogan, and more Hogan. Lacing up your shoes, you feel it will be necessary to dig your game out of the dirt.

Designers are eager to improve standards for golfers, not only by building superb courses, but also by persuading players by stealth to practice. Aside from the driving range, facilities include two chipping greens, two sand bunkers, and a large putting green with an elephantine hump.

The 342-yard first forces a carry over water, the distant greenside pot bunker a good aiming tool. The lake parallels the fairway at right and juts in front of the green. Hole two has a 50-yard ribbon trap to the right at driving distance. A hidden gully runs in front of the raised green, further protected by sand at the rear right quarter. A solid one-shot is the 183-yard third. Two imposing bunkers wrap around the green, which falls away to the rear.

Number four is a majestic hole, fit to grace Augusta National. This par-5 double dogleg through trees requires a fade from the tee, as the fairway shapes downhill. On the second shot, position is all. A mid-iron should be sufficient to reach the ankle of the hole, leaving a short iron into an innocent toenail green. Sand guards the front left, and mounds ring the rear.

An uphill fade at the 390-yard fifth is the favored shape for the tee shot. Trees to the right have water behind. The green sits above the fairway, sloping from rear right to front left; clubbing up is a wise move for a rear pin position. The sixth doglegs left over a sandy waste area, with the right of the fairway giving easier access to the large green. A horizontal ridge sheds forward and backward.

Fit to grace Augusta National.

Pots and shallow bunkers pepper the green entrance.

Hardest of the par 3s, the seventh plays across water 175 yards to the flag. A liberal placement of bunkers on both sides puts pressure on par-saving up and down. Eight runs straight 410 yards, with fairway bunkers at the landing area on both sides. Another bunker drapes the left side of the green; the rear is semicircled by oaks. On the ninth, a par 5 of 512 yards, most players will need to lay up with their second shot, as a lake cuts in front of the green from 140 yards. A bailout fairway lies to the right for those lacking the confidence or ability to clear the water.

Live oaks adorned with Spanish moss frame most holes on the back nine. They discreetly mask what little housing surrounds the club. Number ten's fairway narrows as the hole slides right. Large free-form bunkers protect the green at left, right, and rear. The eleventh has a ribbon bunker running 50 yards along mounding to the left of the landing area. The green also has sand to the left in a flashed bunker and a pot bunker on a raised mound. The putting surface has a right-center mound, a useful target if the pin is at back left.

Twelve doglegs 378 yards downhill and to the right. Big boys trying to cut the corner over trees will need a lot of height and length to clear them. The sensible way is aiming for the apex and then a mid-iron downhill approach.

The green appears tiny, thanks to large bunkers on either side narrowing the opening.

Thirteen should be a breeze, only 154 yards with water behind and sand hazards squeezing the target. I putted early one morning with dew soaking the grass. Everything broke to the front left quarter, and my ball ran as if on glass.

The fourteenth measures 520 yards. The four par 5s at Bloomingdale aren't automatic two-shot givens for strong players. Design forces golfers to think back from the green. Here, for instance, a 300-yard drive will end up in water. A pond sits like a sinkhole 200 yards from the green. A three-lobed bunker waits at greenside right, and the runway entrance is a mere 9 yards wide.

Fifteen is a gift, 402 yards with no fairway hazards. Sixteen is another par-5 beauty; long and left gives perfect position along the fairway chute. The dilemma comes with the second shot: water must be carried, also pot bunkers. For those of us playing this 488-yarder as a three-shot hole, two bunkers guard the entrance to the second landing area. From 100 yards in, pots and shallow bunkers pepper the entrance to a two-tier green that falls to the left. During construction a family of raccoons lived in the tree behind the green. They were swiftly adopted as mascots and incorporated into the club logo.

The last hole requires only 175 yards off the tee. From here it angles left with a forced carry of 150 yards over wetland. The green gathers to the front left. As I gathered my things and left, Bloomingdale had me dreaming of a single-digit handicap.

The Claw at USF

4202 East Fowler Avenue, Tampa 33620
(813) 632-6893
www.theclawatusf.org

Green fee: $52

Architect: William Mitchell, 1968
Par 71
Gold yardage 6,288; course rating 71.9; slope rating 125
Yellow yardage 5,353; course rating 70.9; slope rating 115

Directions: From I-75 exit 266, go west on Fletcher Avenue 3.4 miles. At 46th Street turn right; entrance is on right in 0.3 miles.

From I-275 exit 52, go east on Fletcher Avenue 2.8 miles. At 46th Street turn left; entrance is on right in 0.3 miles.

Varsity sports teams at the University of South Florida are known as the Bulls, and signs in the neighborhood proclaim this is Bull Country. David Sacks, a 1983 graduate, first donned a bull costume and entertained USF sports fans during time-outs. The mascot did push-ups, shadowboxed, and hoisted a Sun Doll cheerleader on his shoulders, carrying her around the Sun Dome to the theme tune from the *Rocky* movies. This is how the bull came to be known as Rocky and why the Claw's clubhouse grill is so named.

Jim Fee, director of golf, nurtures budding talent, ensuring placement in the top 20 percent of 380 national golf programs. Early spring draws participation from competitive universities such as Kansas, Texas, Ohio, and Tennessee to the USF Invitational Intercollegiate Championship. Ah youth, it's not what it used to be; playing a university course brings back days when limbs were lithe and pace was brisk.

The Claw has tight fairways, small, raised greens (averaging 3,500 square feet), and immense bunkers. I met Tom Bremer, an alumnus from 1972, who said: "If you can score here, you can score anywhere." He admits the course frustrated him so much as a student that he stopped playing for years, but he still carries a handy six handicap.

Trees wreathed in Spanish moss.

The first fairway is narrow and runs through oak trees. The green has a forgiving opening and falls away sharply to the rear. Large lobe bunkers sit at each side. Number two returns parallel to the first, 70 yards shorter and easier; a pot bunker sits greenside right. Things spice up at the third, a 496-yard par 5 into a tunnel of oaks. The fairway runs only eighteen paces wide for a hundred yards through the landing area. Water and a large bunker 75 yards out cover the left approach. The raised green tilts forward, a last sand hazard at the front right. Three is rated hardest hole at the Claw.

The fourth doglegs uphill to the right; this hole is always climbing. The green complex drops off steeply at the rear. A generous collar separates two

Shake hands with the Claw.

bunkers on either side of the putting surface. The fifth is a one-shot hole, 145 yards downhill, the flag protected on both sides by sand. Next, a crescent fairway bends all the way around a lake to the left. This is a true three-shot hole for the average player. From the safe (right) side, a sizeable greenside bunker dogs the approach. Another hazard on the left is even bigger but unseen until too late.

Seven elbows left 410 yards, all the trouble on that side being thicket, trees, and water. Two grass hollows front the platform green; a pot bunker lies to the right. The putting surface falls forwards and slips away to the rear. The ninth tee shot need be no longer than 230 yards. At the 150-yard marker a creek cuts across the hole, which angles right to one of the Claw's larger greens. This sheds predominantly right from a central crown.

The back nine has a distinctly swampy feel; this half joins more than 500 acres of wetlands running eastward to abut the Hillsborough River. It's not unusual to see deer grazing early in the morning about the track.

The tenth doglegs right through a procession of mature oaks. From the outer angle 200 yards remain to the pin. Bunkers at both sides of the cornflake green allow a mere eight yards of runway entrance.

Water is the main feature on the eleventh and one that had me scratching my head to do the math. The hole measures 345 yards. A drive of 170 yards is required to clear pond one, while pond two starts at 130 yards to go. A 25-yard wide trap guards the green frontage with a tiny ramp at the left. The putting surface falls away to the right.

One of the more scenic holes, the 151-yard twelfth is also the easiest. From the tee the green appears wide and shallow but is false fronted to the right. Thirteen hugs a lake in the manner of six but crawls right instead of left. Players with less distance should consider a layup with the second shot, as a creek runs across the fairway. Played too long and right, a ball will end in the pond and in the company of alligators.

The fourteenth is a tight par 5 and gives the Claw its name. A 240-yard tee shot reaches the elbow of the hole. With 250 yards remaining, swamp occupies a fair portion. The green is tilted left to right, like a small mirror held in fingertips to catch the light. Unless confident with a draw, try three 5-irons to get home. I often hear the advice to treat a par 5 as three par 3s in a row.

Fifteen plays straight, except for a pond at the 100-yard marker. The platform green is guarded on both sides by bunkers. The 168-yard sixteenth has a wide bunker running across the front and more sand at the sides. Tom Bremer said, "Once you've made it past sixteen, you've made it." The last two holes are parallel, one playing up and the other down. Seventeen's green has a large pot at the front. Eighteen, a 392-yard slight dogleg right, has two pots at the front and a punchbowl surface.

You just shook hands with the Claw.

Fox Hollow

10050 Robert Trent Jones Parkway, Trinity 34655
(727) 376-6333
www.golfthefox.com

Green fee: $85

Architects: Robert Trent Jones and Roger Rulewich, 1994
Par 71
Blue yardage 6,801; course rating 73.2; slope rating 127
Red yardage 5,203; course rating 70.3; slope rating 127

Directions: From 589 (Suncoast Parkway) exit 19, go west on 54 (Gunn Highway) 4.5 miles. At Trinity Boulevard turn left; entrance (Tamarind Boulevard) is on left in 2.3 miles.

From 19 [55] in Tarpon Springs, take Keystone Road east 3.0 miles. At East Lake Road turn left. Go 1.2 miles to Trinity Boulevard and turn right. In 2.2 miles, at Robert Trent Jones Parkway, turn right; entrance is on right in 1.1 miles.

Eli Fox purchased Crump Soda in the mid-nineteenth century unaware he would inspire a trio of golf courses and their nattily attired wily mascot. A. R. "Bill" Sandri left the granite quarries of Barre, Vermont, in 1929 and went into the fuel distribution business in Massachusetts. His son, William, attended the Wharton School of Business, graduating alongside Donald Trump. In 1978 Crumpin-Fox Club was built in Bernardston, Massachusetts, home of the Crump Fox Soda Company. In 1987 William Sandri purchased Crumpin-Fox Club, with renovations by Robert Trent Jones. Three courses now operate under the Fox logo.

Near Tampa it's Fox Hollow. This happens to be the last golf course designed by Robert Trent Jones Inc. that opened while the company remained a going concern. Roger Rulewich was Jones's chief designer for more than thirty years and must be given credit for Fox Hollow.

Head professional Dave Stewart has a keen interest in golf literature, and I succumbed to my shopping vice, leaving with a book by A. W. Tillinghast. I was put in the care of Dave's most earnest assistant, Peter Egazarian, a dedicated professional in his early twenties who works at another Fox property during the summer months.

On the opening hole, a short par 4, 206 yards carries bunkers at the left landing area. To guard the green, a front pot bunker accompanies mounds at the rear, where there's considerable drop-off. On the second, a lake sits to the left with staggered cross bunkers left and then right. The best play is 180 yards to the right of the first bunker, then a mid-iron in. Fox Hollow greens are full of undulation and disperse balls every which way.

The third is a 429-yard par 4 with water left and out-of-bounds right. From the wavy peak-and-trough fairway a confident player's second shot needs to fly a greenside trap. Peter pointed out the rear-right pin position and warned me a 2-iron from two hundred yards won't stop on a dime. Those of us not blessed with length will do better laying up to pitching distance.

Hole four, this side's only par 5, doglegs left around a lake. Aiming bunkers indicate the first landing area, and more bunkers feature at the second landing area and greenside. An elevated target, if missed to the left, has the player recovering from a deep gully.

Thirteen's green.

Ibis and sandhill cranes pecked their way around the tee box, while a great blue heron fished in the lake at the fifth. On this neat 178-yard par 3, water plays all the way left and fronts the green, where two pot bunkers give added protection. The putting surface slopes right to left. Peter pronounced it "a very fair hole."

Cross bunkers needing a 270-yard clearance are directly in line with the green at six. The sensible play is a driver or 3-wood to the left-hand side, then an approach to the green, which angles left. From a central ridge it falls quickly to front right and softly back left. Seven is of similar difficulty to six, with its green angled the other way. Tee shot placement left of fairway bunkers leaves optimal approach in a fade to the deep and narrow target, avoiding forward pot bunkers.

Number eight is a one-shot hole into a green that breaks like a peace sign: rear right, rear left, and forward from the center. Nine is a classic par 4 of 403 yards. Fairway bunkers gather anything wide from 200 to 288 yards off the tee. Two bunkers squeeze the green entrance, and a pot to the right is thrown in for good measure.

Although Fox Hollow is semiprivate, 65 percent of the rounds are by non-members. Despite property development, there are no immediate plans to make the course exclusive to members and guests. In summer 2005, smaller homes started at $400,000, but living beside the tenth fairway cost a cool $1.4 million.

As well as out-of-bounds left, ten has water off the tee and right. A lake wraps around fairway bunkers and covers the front of the green, which sheds both ways from a center seam. Eleven's tee shot has a 204-yard carry over water. For the second at this par 5, Peter advised playing to favored wedge or mid-iron distance, depending upon ability. The green is tucked away to the left, with substantial fairway and greenside bunkering covering the approach.

The twelfth is stunning in its simplicity: par 3 of 202 yards, a ridge in the center of the green, one pot bunker bang in front. No trees or waste area to prettify or distract—just tee, target, and hazard.

Thirteen is a perimeter hole, but water moves the fairway away from the road for the final 160 yards. Far right gives the best entrance to the green. Fourteen, at 465 yards, is a driver and 3-wood for some; many of us are forced to ponder the three-shot approach. The receptive green's front right quarter spills into a sand hazard.

The key to the par-5 fifteenth, which doglegs right around water from crook of knee to turned-in foot, is placement of the second shot. A remaining "par 3" over water and a front pot bunker is ideal from around 130 yards. The par-3 sixteenth imitates this approach and hazard but extends it by 20 yards.

A spreading oak off the tee is the first expression of the home hole. The fairway is a long peninsula framed by a smile of water (see color plate 14). Peter informed me his play at eighteen is a 2-iron and then a 2-iron. I peeled myself away from the cart, wondering in which lifetime I would be able to hit a 2-iron well enough to attempt it twice.

Mangrove Bay

875 62nd Avenue NE, St. Petersburg 33702
(727) 893-7800
www.stpete.org/rec/golf_pages/mangrove.htm

Green fee: $39

Architect: Bill Amick, 1978
Par 72
White yardage 6,112; course rating 68.8; slope rating 114
Red yardage 5,176; course rating 69.7; slope rating 115

*Directions: From I-275 exit 26, take 54th Avenue east 1.9 miles. At 1st Street N,
turn left and go 0.5 miles. At 62nd Avenue NE, turn right and go 0.6 miles to
Cardinal Road. Turn left; entrance is ahead in 0.2 miles.*

A leaf falls from a mangrove tree in coastal wetlands. Bacteria and fungi grow
on the dead leaf and are eaten by shrimp and small fish, which in turn become
the diet of larger fish. Predatory seabirds feed on fish; humans, too, catch and
savor this protein provider. Take away the mangrove, and the rug is pulled from
under the pyramid balanced *en pointe*. In 1969 two scientists at the University
of Miami discovered this detrital food chain by studying Florida's mangrove
swamps.

Mangrove Bay gives an opportunity to play golf within this ecological won-
derland. The City of St. Petersburg runs the facility, an early example of landfill
conversion. The original routing was given a facelift in 1998, and Cypress Links,
a handsome 9-hole par-3 course, was added the year before. This executive
layout was by Roger Parks, one of the original construction team. Remodeling
included several lakes. The lake dirt was then used to create mounding, since
no muck can be removed from the site. Aerial photographs show it treeless in
the early years; now the course is gaining definition with cypress and palms,
notably Canary Island date palms as 150-yard markers on every hole.

To begin, aim left of the first fairway bunker on a short par 4. Two bunkers
bolster the left of the green, which tilts forward, and a pot bunker sits lonely on
the right. Mangrove swamp lines the way left on the par-5 second, the hardest

hole on this nine, though five and six are a meaty combination. Cross bunkers are placed at the second landing area, and one greenside bunker to the right. The putting surface gathers to a depression at rear left.

Three is a one-shot hole of 127 yards. The green is guarded by bunkers at front left and rear; the front half falls toward the tee. If you notice an agricultural aroma on these first holes, be aware a waste treatment plant is across the street. I found no unpleasant odors from here on, aside from my own game.

The fifth elbows to the left, 362 yards in distance. A stand of palms and a fairway bunker block the line to the pin. Two bunkers cover the right-hand approach line 125 yards from the target, and water lies at the extreme right. The green tilts rear left to front right.

Six is a great hole and greatly underrated. A bunker guards the landing area 230 yards off the tee, leaving 250 yards to go. Cross hazards block the line to the green, forcing second-shot placement to the right. No matter how far right you play, a trio of bunkers obstructs the entrance to the target. A sparse stand of trees shuts off play to the left. The angled green slopes left to right if viewed from the fairway, or back to front if seen from the runway.

Seven curls around a lake to the left. Its coin-shaped green tilts to the front left quarter. This is where I met Chester, now in his early eighties and a volun-

Canary Island date palms as 150-yard markers.

Ringed at the rear by palms and pines.

teer ranger. Chester remembers an eight-dollar green fee and no cart paths. He pointed out an osprey's nest on top of a floodlight pole on the driving range, and wildlife galore: turkey buzzards, hawks and eagles, otters and raccoons.

To the right of the par-3 eighth is mangrove swamp where many a stray ball lies uncollected—cottonmouths and rattlesnakes keep away the wise. Chester also alerted me to the pygmy rattlers. "They won't kill you, but you'll be real sick for days." I wasn't keen to discover if pygmy rattlers were a species apart or merely rattlesnakes yet to reach maturity. This, Reader, I will leave to your own research.

The ninth green has a ledge at rear left and sheds to the front right quarter; two pots right and a bunker left afford the protection on this par 4 of 379 yards. Stay away from the right side on the tenth: no trouble for your ball, just an increased chance of being hit by a hook from the driving range. The twelfth angles left along a line of mangroves. An aiming pot bunker sits 260 yards from the tee, leaving 150 yards to go. Fade in the approach to the deep and narrow green, but beware the small pot bunker at greenside right.

Fourteen is a 485-yard par 5 with a wide fairway. Bunkers begin 230 yards from the tee box and stagger the remaining distance. The green is well protected by sand and ringed at the rear by Washingtonia palms and young slash pines. The fifteenth is a one-shot hole of 180 yards with swampy water on both sides. A receptive green slopes from back left to front right, where a bunker awaits.

Club selection is especially important on sixteen: water cuts across the fairway 225 yards from the white tees. From the dry land across the hazard the hole rises to an open green with bunkers at the rear. The putting surface, like a scallop shell, gathers to a cup at front center.

First- and second-shot landing areas affect the par-5 seventeenth. A large lace-edged bunker covers the left side of the green, which tilts to that direction. The home hole plays 381 yards around water. The fairway, undulated as an unmade bed, leads to the raised, forward-sloping green. The front is guarded by three of fifty-seven bunkers on the course.

Bill Amick is renowned for his designs on landfill and is considered the premier exponent of this art. Mangrove Bay is an intelligent use of derelict land and solidly utilitarian in character. This is fun golf, affordable golf, an integral part of the Gulf Coast chain.

For more information on mangroves, check out www.mangrove.org.

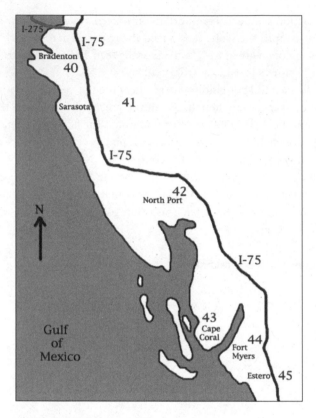

Gulf Coast, Bradenton and South

40 River Run
41 Oak Ford
42 Bobcat Trail
43 Coral Oaks
44 Eastwood
45 Stoneybrook

River Run Golf Links

1801 27th Street E, Bradenton 34208
(941) 708-8459
www.riverrungolflinks.com

Green fee: $38

Architect: Ward Northrup, 1987
Par 70
Blue yardage 6,293; course rating 70.9; slope rating 131
Red yardage 4,709; course rating 66.9; slope rating 119

Directions: From I-75 exit 220, west on 64 (Manatee Avenue) 3.7 miles. At 27th Street E turn left 1.0 mile, entrance is on left.

Sharing adjacent riparian rights with River Run is an orange grove. Oranges have been cultivated in Florida for five hundred years; grapefruit was introduced only two centuries ago. Freak winter freezes forced fruit growers and their groves south. Production increased from a million boxes per annum in 1865 to current levels of well over 200 million boxes. Today citrus is a $9 billion industry. Alongside the state's usual departments, Florida even has its own Department of Citrus.

Back in 1939, Rosa and Willie Mixon purchased a 20-acre grove and sold oranges from a roadside stand. Mail order proved the making of Mixon's Fruit Farm. Today, visitors take tours of the processing plant at the 350-acre grove, still managed by the family. River Run borders the fruit farm to the north, and has some orange trees of its own.

It won't escape your notice that River Run shares a car park with McKechnie Field, home of the Pittsburgh Pirates during spring training. For the benefit of readers unfamiliar with the baseball calendar, this preseason season involves teams from the Frozen North and Shivering South spending six weeks in Florida, training and playing in the so-called Grapefruit League. Boston's Red Sox train in Fort Myers, the New York Yankees in Tampa, the Cincinnati Reds in Sarasota, and the Baltimore Orioles in Fort Lauderdale. Avid fans arrange their winter vacations around games; tickets cost the equivalent of a large bucket of

First choice on the back nine.

range balls. Spring training started in the 1880s, and the league was well under way by the early twentieth century. Pirates coming off practice are known to swap bats for clubs and catch twilight tee times.

A tight core layout, the front nine has the only noticeable elevation changes and a little more room to spare; the back forms two deflated loops folding in on each other. Already the established venue for Bradenton's City Championship and the City Seniors Championship, River Run primarily offers fun golf at a fair price and is ideal for the recreational golfer. Visitors returning for the first time since renovation will find the nines reversed and the greens in better shape. Jed Azinger and Gordon Lewis remodeled River Run in summer 2005. All tee boxes were moved to beef up the length, and the corridor shared by holes four and eight was adjusted to answer safety concerns.

The first fairway (beyond McKechnie Field's third base) tightens at driving distance. Bunkers rim the green at left, right, and rear. From an elevated tee, the 525-yard second is the longest hole on the course. Mangroves lining the right-hand side and a fairway bunker are the hazards. Keeping left for both opening shots is the wise play. A pond 120 yards from the flag and a large tree shading the green shut off approach from the right. The putting surface slopes forward, guarded heavily by sand at the left and rear.

The third plays along a chute to a forward-sloping green. The green was shortened (thus lengthening the hole) and a voluminous greenside bunker partially filled in.

A new tee at four prevents a drive all the way to the green. Shooting to the corner where the fairway angles right, 210 yards away, leaves a short iron in. The green is protected at the front and falls away to the left. Five doglegs left ninety degrees; another tee shot of 210–220 yards is ideal. Across a brook, 150 yards distant, two shallow bunkers lobe the flat-faced green.

Seven slides downhill to a circular green with a sand hazard at the right-hand side. At the 421-yard ninth, a ribbon of sand runs left on the approach, and two right bunkers protect the green.

Faced with a choice at the 361-yard tenth, the player either lays up, leaving a shot over water, or goes longer, left of an oak at the inner angle of the dogleg, ensuring a dry approach. The small raised green tilts forward. A mangrove wall runs left the length of the eleventh, and water lies to the right on the approach. Sprawling across the runway is a bunker containing an island of grass.

On twelve a forced 190-yard carry leaves 160 yards to a coin-shaped green with a rear bunker. The next doglegs to the right with a bunker greenside left.

Sixteen's green.

I saw slice potential here in an orange tree beside the green. From a distance I mistook fallen fruit for a yellow golf ball. I made a mental note to schedule a visit to the optician.

Fourteen plays over water 148 yards to a forward-sloping green. The dogleg fifteenth needs a draw to avoid the bunker at the fairway's right. A greenside bunker contains its own stand of palm trees, an imitation of the classic desert island cartoon.

Sixteen turns sharply right with 100 yards to go. A 230-yard drive to the left side of the fairway leaves perfect position. The approach must carry a bunker at the entrance to the green. Seventeen is a textbook par 3, slightly downhill to a generous green with two large, lobed bunkers.

The last is a strong hole, narrowing off the tees with bunkers around the 200-yard marker. To the right, water and trees mask the green. Place the second shot to favored wedge distance, since the green requires aerial approach. Bunkers surround the putting surface, which sheds to the left.

Golf, orange groves, and baseball's spring training are three of Florida's defining characteristics—all originally imports by visitors. How appropriate to have them sit side by side so charmingly by the Bradenton River.

- - - - - - - - - - - -

41

Oak Ford Golf Club

1552 Palm View Road, Sarasota 34240
(941) 371-3680
www.oakfordgolfclub.com

Green fee: $55

Architect: Ron Garl, 1989

Blue/Red	Oaks+Palms	Myrtle+Oaks	Palms+Myrtle
Par	72	72	72
Yardage	6,230/5,054	6,287/5,085	6,321/5,051
Course rating	69.7/68.8	70.0/67.6	70.5/68.1
Slope rating	124/116	123/116	126/118

Directions: From I-75 exit 210, take 780 (Fruitville Road) east 9.0 miles. At Oakford Road turn right and go 1.2 miles to Palm View Road. Turn right; entrance is 0.6 miles ahead.

A blend of swamp, farmland, and a stretch of open, treeless holes makes this 27-hole mélange of golf styles and atmospheres a delight for the most discerning palate.

Oak Ford was conceived as a private club but never reached its maximum potential. Maybe the swamp dragged it back or the nine-mile commute from the interstate had members wishing to save gas and save the planet. In 2003 the Schwartz family purchased the property and opened it for daily fee players. Sons Dusty and Trace, installed as general manager and superintendent respectively, ensure it is given care and attention worthy of a family member. No rookies to the golf business, the younger Schwartzes worked previously for the TPC at Sawgrass, and the family already owned a course in Indiana.

Advice from starters, pro shop staff, and players suggests no superior nine or combination. The course called Palms winds through a swamp, with open holes toward home. Myrtle provides the toughest finish with two penal holes. Oaks is spooky in the first half and includes a three-hole, almost links-like corridor toward the end. My preference would be Oaks and Palms, a spot of lunch, and then attack Myrtle.

Palms

A ribbon bunker occupies mounding to the left of the first fairway. The mounds curl around the rear of the green, which slopes forward and splits left and right. Number two is a penal one-shot, the top of the flagstick just visible 171 yards away over swamp. The green is 18 yards deep by 30 yards wide, with a collecting bowl at center left. On the way to the next tee, the mangrove boardwalk has speed bumps allowing ample time to admire sandhill cranes and ibis.

Hole five is only 334 yards long, but interrupted twice by threads of wetland across the fairway; a good drive should take both out of play. A cape bunker covers the entrance, while overshooting the green leaves an unplayable lie in tangled scrub behind. Six is the difficult one on Palms: 507 yards with a cross bunker 100 yards from the pin that continues to greenside. Mounding at the rear frames and elevates the green.

The seventh plays around a lake. At 300 yards a monster drive could reach the target, and a prevailing wind from the right quarter helps. Two enormous amoeba-shaped bunkers trap anything short and right. For those making their way in two shots or more, the fairway rises gently to a forward-pitching green.

Amoeba-shaped bunkers.

With water running left, the eighth has a tricky tee shot. A 175-yard drill down the middle is safest, leaving 150 yards to an unprotected cornflake green. Three companions tried to go longer off the tee, and all ended up in cross bunkering to the right.

The finish is strategic. Monsters should leave their drivers in the bag: the 292-yard par 4 needs a 3-wood or long-iron tee shot to reach wedge distance. Water lies left and gives the small target a peninsula effect. A large live oak stands to the right surrounded by sand.

Oaks

The four holes from number two onward are my favorite stretch. Through moss-draped oaks, around lake and swamp with alligators and overhead a circling eagle, the landscape seemed so pregnant with peril that I half expected to see Vincent Price lurking around the tee box.

A drive of 250 yards should reach the widest part of the fairway on the third. A lake inhibits the second shot, so break the remaining 240 yards into the happiest combination. A cluster of bunkers protects the green's right side. Hole four is a par 3 of 202 yards. The putting surface has a mound at the center, but tilts mainly forward. The last ghostly hole has a small landing area to the right as the fairway creeps and crawls around water on the left. One of the smaller greens, the target is unprotected except by scrub to the left and behind.

The remaining holes play in open land. To reach the par-5 eighth requires two hefty shots. Its raised green is tucked to the right, mounded to the right and bunkered left. The ninth green lies at the end of a waste bunker inhibiting approach from the right-hand side. The green slopes from rear right to front left.

Myrtle

Myrtle provides the toughest test. The opening tee shot is played through a narrow chute of trees and over swamp to the fairway. The green is an unguarded finger, 40 yards deep and 11 yards wide. A par 5 and two par 4s follow in grinding fashion.

Five, at 134 yards with front bunkers, is a brief respite before four tough closing holes. The sixth requires a tee shot of 175 yards to clear the water. From here 200 yards remain to the pin, the first half over swamp. Forward tee players have an option to make this a par-3 of 135 yards. It really is a hole made of two par 3s—most likely environmental issues halted any incursion into the swamp on the approach. Oak Ford has an arboreal signature of live oak ringed by saw

Oak Ford's arboreal signature.

palmetto and hung with Spanish moss; the waste bunker on seven displays a prime example.

The ninth has risk and reward similar to six, with a 160-yard forced carry over water and then the choice of laying up or being a hero. From 125 yards out, the carry is over small palms to a raised green with a pot bunker at the front. The green breaks downhill to the left.

Yes, best save Myrtle for last—or better still, for a 9-hole scramble.

42

Bobcat Trail Golf Club

1350 Bobcat Trail, North Point 34288
(941) 429-0500
www.bobcattrailgc.com

Green fee: $80

Architects: Bob Tway and Lee Singletary, 1998
Par 71
Bobcat gold tees (10–20 handicap men):
Yardage 6,242; course rating 70.8; slope rating 130
Hawk silver tees (0–25 handicap ladies):
Yardage 5,271; course rating 71.3; slope rating 123

Directions: From I-75 exit 179, go south on Toledo Blade Boulevard 3.2 miles; entrance is on left.

Bobcat Trail came recommended by James Kennedy, a teaching professional from Connecticut, and I welcomed his advice. PGA Tour player Bob Tway and Lee Singletary produced a design to keep better players on their toes, afford a fair test of skill for the mid-handicapper, and give happy hackers a roller coaster ride. The Cat's fairways are forgivingly wide in the tee-shot landing area, but tend to narrow from there on. If its bunkers wore T-shirts, they'd be size 2XL. The greens are from the school of Dr. Alister MacKenzie. No flat plates these, no crowns with subtle breaks, no curling cornflakes; the Cat's putting surfaces resemble Salvador Dalí's melting watches.

Receiving a complimentary sleeve of balls in exchange for my green fee was a tad disconcerting. Gazing at the aqua range, I wondered whether this was a lake course and whether one sleeve would be sufficient. The pro shop staff assured me it was a promotional gift. Water is a constant at the Cat, mostly as a lateral hazard, as a forced carry only on a handful of holes.

Trees are the hazard at the first, running the length of the right-hand side. The tee shot should cut away from a fairway bunker 130 yards from the target. The green is bell-shaped, and its top step flows forward to the lower, outer rim.

Number three—strategically a tiny nightmare.

The second is a one-shot hole of 177 yards with a pot bunker at front left. A cloverleaf green slips away to the edge of each petal.

Three is strategically a tiny nightmare. The approach is covered by a slash pine at left, a greenside bunker at right, and an inlet of water before the pine. The shallow, oval green has a center parting and sheds balls predominantly downhill to the left. On the fourth, cross bunkers and a gully occupy the right-hand side from tee to target.

My playing partner, Jed from Minnesota, made par at the fifth and was only +2 at the turn. In his early forties, he resembles actor Tim Robbins and carries a six handicap. He hit drives of 250 yards all day from the back tees. He has two rules concerning golf: never leave home any earlier to play than for work, and don't play when it's below fifty degrees Fahrenheit.

Jed's prowess is due to his father's goading. "Dad was a frustrated golfer, he came to the game in his thirties. He told my brothers and me the only sport we'd participate in past our forties would be golf. He didn't want us to be miserable golfing adults." Jed has broken 70 a couple or three times, but is happy shooting in the mid-70s and only slightly miserable scoring 80-plus. "I come to a golf course to relax," he says. "This is recreation. Some people attach too much importance to their game—they get so tense."

The sixth, the solitary par 5 on the front nine, has bunkers to the left with 330 yards to go, bunkers to the right with 160 to go, and an approach over water to a very undulating green. Seven's green, like an old felt hat, twists down at front left and falls at rear right; a pond makes the 141 yards more intimidating.

Water forces a carry from the tee on the ninth, a 428-yard hole sliding left around the aqua range. Aim right of the Tway Tree in line with the fairway bunker 266 yards from the tee. The green pitches forward to front center; bunkers are placed behind and left.

Number eleven, a 126-yard par 3, has a green with gathering bowl at the front. Our tee shots stayed on the higher, rear portion, failing to roll down to the pin position: Bobcat's greens had been sanded that morning.

Two difficult holes follow. Twelve's tee shot is across a neck of land with water on both sides. A drive of 225 yards finds the widest part of the fairway. Water continues on the right. The target is guarded by a pot at front left and a cape bunker behind. From a central ridge the putting surface sheds to front right and rear left.

Jed launched a drive down the middle at the 493-yard thirteenth. With around 220 yards remaining, he was in two minds whether or not to go for it. I

Bobcat's aqua range.

reminded him *Tin Cup* was just a movie, that this green also had water in front, and that its being elevated made it that little bit longer. He hit his second to wedge distance and two-putted for par. Meanwhile, I had played an unglamorous triple-5-iron strategy, chipped on from the left rough, and three-putted for double bogey. Nobody said it was going to be easy.

Fifteen is a short par 4, the fairway split by water off the tee. Pot bunkers protect the front of the green with heavily bunkered mounding at the rear. The putting surface spills forward, and my uphill putt was always going to be too short.

The final pair keep the pressure on for difficulty. Seventeen curls left around a lake for 463 yards. The fairway slopes toward the water, which cuts off the green at the approach. A testy par 4 finishes proceedings.

Some better players find it debilitating to play with hackers. Duffers, on the other hand, can raise their game alongside the more skillful. Jed dropped four strokes over the final five holes. I apologized for dragging his game down. He blamed tiredness and trying to protect his score. Diplomacy done with, he finished at 78. My score was a good deal higher.

43

Coral Oaks Golf Course

1800 NW 28th Avenue, Cape Coral 33993
(239) 573-3100

Green fee: $57

Architect: Arthur Hills, 1988
Par 72
Blue yardage 6,078; course rating 70.0; slope rating 133
Red yardage 4,803; course rating 68.3; slope rating 115

Directions: From I-75 exit 143, go west on 78 (Bayshore Road, which becomes Pine Island Road) 15.7 miles. At 765 (Burnt Store Road) turn right (north), go 3.7 miles to Van Buren Road, and turn right again. In 0.5 miles, at NW 28th Avenue, turn right; entrance is 0.2 mile ahead.

A sign by the first tee declares what all golfers know in their hearts to be a moral truth: "No Mulligans." Many of life's little hooks and shanks make us want to wipe the slate clean and begin again, but we all know the score. If I ignore one or more of my fluffs, whiffs, dibs, chunks, hooks, or slices, then I am playing another game and it is not called golf. In this case, getting groups away in good time is the priority. A par-5 opening hole of 504 yards can have three groups in play. A large bunker halfway down the fairway and a deep pot bunker at the front of the green are the only hazards to halt a smooth start.

After clearing 160 yards of water at the second, the hole rises gently to an unguarded, forward-sloping green. The third has water on the left, and the fairway narrows considerably from the 100-yard marker. Mounds and a bunker protect the right side, and the green leans to the lake. On four, a par 4 of 402 yards, a lone cabbage palm stands in the middle of the fairway. A greenside bunker on the right could ruin par here, as the green slopes to the front left quarter.

Any suggestion this is an easy track with open fairways is dispelled by the remaining holes on this side. The fifth is a short par 4, only 271 yards, but a forced carry over water except from the forward tees. From the blue tees I was reminded of a line from my school hymnal: "There is a green hill far away." The putting table sits high with surrounding mounding; three bunkers below provide potential punishment for those who dare to treat it as a one-shot hole.

Trees frame the par-3 sixth. The green is 38 yards deep by 14 yards wide and flows to the front right. A pot bunker collects anything short of the generous target. Seven plays through a chute of tall trees toward a fairway bunker at driving distance. The hole slides left from the 150-yard marker; trees and bunkering protect a left-side approach. To the right, humps and hollows pitch and toss access to an elevated pin.

Hole eight is a juicy 187 yards, with water covering the left and front of the green. The only bailout is the drop area to the right. The green, of course, pulls everything toward the water. A dramatic par 5 completes the front half. On the second shot from the wide fairway, a large bunker blocks the entrance to the green 75 yards out. Mounding along the right side will likely kick second shots into the sand. A bunker sits greenside left; the putting surface has three collecting areas, front right, center left, and to the rear.

Some courses switch nines and it doesn't amount to much in the grand scheme of things. I have heard of courses occasionally played backward as well as forward. One of golf's design mantras is to start easy and get harder as players warm up, then sting them with drama at the finish. The nines at Coral

Big bunker off the ninth—originally the eighteenth.

The eighteenth—originally the ninth.

Oaks have been reversed, so the turn seems easier than the start. This is of little interest to most, of some import to the purist, and one can only imagine how it affects the designer. When reading a four-page article it is folly to start halfway through, read to the end, and then return to page one to find out what happened in the beginning. Three, four, one, two is not a happy progression ... unless it's your golf score.

Thus the tenth is a straight par 4 of medium difficulty, and perfect for an opening gambit. Eleven, a par 5 of 495 yards, is the hardest hole at Coral Oaks. Water takes the right side with 220 yards remaining; a ribbon bunker runs parallel for the final 150 yards. A spreading live oak blocks the left approach. When initially played as the second hole, eleven proved to hold up play considerably. The par-3 twelfth compounded the delay, hence the switch of nines.

The next trio are par 4s running along the eastern perimeter of the property. They must have been a gift when routing center lines. Beware the water on thirteen: unseen from the tee, it cuts in front of the green.

The three closing holes are like two entrees followed by a scoop of vanilla ice cream. The sixteenth is a par 5 of 488 yards. Two cabbage palms stand 200 yards from the target. Play to their right to get a view of the green, tucked away to the left. Scrub occupies the left-hand portion of the approach, and a long greenside bunker rims the flat putting surface.

Seventeen looks like the home hole. The fairway leads straight to the car park and clubhouse with conspicuous bunkers arranged before—a beautiful optical illusion, as here the hole turns sharply right for another 170 yards. The green is mounded, without bunkers, its three tiers cascading from rear right to front left. The final hole (originally the ninth, and designed to flow to the old tenth, which is now the first) plays behind the clubhouse as an attractive par 3 over water.

Homes around Coral Oaks are set back from the fairways. In general the course has an open feeling and ample elbow room, and the space to swing is matched by the unpretentious character of the growing neighborhood. This public venue should influence the burgeoning locale to the good.

Eastwood Golf Course

4600 Bruce Herd Lane, Fort Myers 33994
(239) 275-4848
www.cityftmyers.com/attractions/golf/eastwood.aspx

Green fee: $60

Architects: Robert von Hagge and Bruce Devlin, 1977
Par 72
Blue yardage 6,772; course rating 72.3; slope rating 130
Red yardage 5,116; course rating 68.9; slope rating 120

Directions: From I-75 South exit 138, go west on 82 (Martin Luther King Jr. Boulevard) 0.5 miles. At Ortiz Avenue turn left; entrance is on right in 1.2 miles.

From I-75 North exit 136, go west on 884 (Colonial Boulevard) 0.4 miles. At Ortiz Avenue turn right; entrance is on left in 0.5 miles.

If it weren't for the lightbulb and the motorcar, Fort Myers might never have graduated from a cattle town. Thomas Edison, inventor of the lightbulb and mentor to Henry Ford, brought his second wife to the town in 1885 and began to winter here regularly. In 1916 Henry Ford moved in next door. The two domiciles are now combined as the Edison Ford Museum, with house, laboratory, and horticultural gardens providing an interesting two-hour diversion. The entrance is canopied by the largest banyan tree in the United States, now spreading more than 400 feet, grown from a sucker brought from India by Harvey Firestone.

The residents of Fort Myers attempted a golf course in 1906. Cyclists found it difficult to pedal their machines through the sand two miles east of the fledgling community, so it was soon abandoned. The year after Henry Ford's arrival, Donald Ross was contracted to build a golf course, which survives today as Fort Myers Country Club, a mile or so south of the Edison Ford Museum along McGregor Boulevard. The first four holes play directly into the morning sun, the last pair on each nine directly into the setting sun. One professional golfer

Defining the corner.

suggested this might be one of Ross's "phoned-in" designs. Nobody I spoke with volunteered information to the contrary.

In 1977 the city got its municipal golf course to the east in the shape of Eastwood. Since it runs through woodlands, no houses surround the fairways, though some modern development has taken place opposite the tenth. Slash pines and palms predominate as vegetation; water comes into play on a few holes. Eighty-five bunkers provide abundant opportunity to play from the sand. While the course is credited as a joint effort of the two architects, it is clear Mr. von Hagge stayed behind after school a little while longer to punish miscreant golfers.

A gentle start is a dogleg to the right. Aim long and left to open up the approach. From the higher portion at rear right, the green slopes to the front left quarter. Another easing-in hole follows. From the tee the fairway appears blocked by sand; in effect, the bunkers are staggered and a narrow gully leads to the green, which gathers to front left.

On three, water lies left and a row of trees lines the other side. Large bunkers are placed at the front of the green on both sides and at rear right. The right side offers meager access along the ground. The first par 3 has a raised green 233 yards away. There's no shame in players deciding to hit from the white tees here;

it's only 165 yards. Take one more club to allow for the elevation, but beware the steep-faced bunker sitting proudly behind the pin. The fifth fairway doglegs right, with mounded ribbon bunkers defining both edges of the curvature. The sand around the green looks dramatic; play safe and worm the ball in to secure par.

Number six is no cakewalk even from the forward tees; from the blues, it's 177 yards of carry over a lake, with sand before and behind the green, which pitches down to the left. If not going for greatness, a small bailout area to the right of the green is an option. Seven plays back around the lake, with mounding and bunkers banking the middle stretch. The approach is across water and a greenside bunker.

Two stiff holes play back to the clubhouse. The eighth is the only par 5 on the front side, a right-angled dogleg with aiming bunkers 230 yards out. The second-shot landing area is hipped by cross bunkers, the green beyond surrounded by sand. The ninth tee shot needs no more than 225 yards to roll short of hazards on both sides. This leaves 144 yards across water to a target triangled by sand.

If you naturally draw the ball, the back nine will be right up your alley. The tenth fairway skirts a lake from tee to landing area, and everything feeds down to the left. The plateau green is heavily bunkered. To quote the useful yardage

A bunker prevents use of the contours.

book: "more balls go into #10 lake than any other!" Eleven also shapes to the left; a ribbon of greenside sand smirks at failed approach shots. The twelfth is the only fairway to move right on the back nine and should guarantee par after a well-placed tee shot. The green at the 204-yard thirteenth has so many breaks, my notebook sketch has arrows pointing in every direction.

The par-5 fourteenth is 573 yards, with bunkers featuring at the right of both landing areas. The putting surface tilts left, toward the water, while a bunker above the green to the right prevents use of the contours. The one-shot fifteenth plays over a lake with bunkers front, right, and rear. The smart money might be in aiming short and right, then rolling the ball up to the hole with the second shot, though this may seem overcautious score-protectionism.

Sixteen is a long, thin par 5. Water and trees flank the left side all the way. Moguls and bunkers line the right-hand side; the target is liberally garnished with bunkers. Seventeen's green is wide and very approachable once you've cleared the hazard halfway down the fairway. A heroic finish calls for a carry over water to the fairway, sliding around the lake to the left. The requisite mounding berm guides us around the corner to the home straight. There's no respite from sand, its presence more marked the closer we come to the hole.

Stoneybrook Golf Course

21253 Stoneybrook Golf Drive, Estero 33928
(239) 948-3933
www.stoneybrookgolffm.com

Green fee: $90

Architects: Jed Azinger and Gordon Lewis, 1999
Par 72
Blue yardage 6,715; course rating 72.3; slope rating 135
Red yardage 4,672; course rating 67.0; slope rating 115

*Directions: From I-75 exit 123, go east on 850 (Corkscrew Road) 0.5 miles;
entrance is on right.*

Bruce K. Harwood II took up the game at four years of age and is now the head golf professional at Stoneybrook. He's been there since groundbreaking, grow-in, and opening in 1999. While on tour, he struck a tree root and damaged tendons in his thumb. His playing career temporarily halted, he turned to management. He's the youngest head professional in the tri-counties of Charlotte, Lee, and Collier.

Walking the course is not an option. Formidable distances separate greens and tees, though golfers of all abilities can play here. Six sets of tees are supplemented by junior tees, which also serve as drop zones for those who never make landfall. Club rental, helpfully, includes a dozen balls and a kit comprising tees, ball marker, and pitch mark repair tool.

Stoneybrook has water on every hole. You're either hitting over water from the tee or trying to avoid it on one side, sometimes two, on occasion three. A time you can gladly hit into the drink is at the driving range. Think of it as preparation for the inevitable. First-time visitors might not be familiar with Florida's aqua ranges, where island targets like green buoys bob in a field of water. Aqua range balls have the same compression and click as an ordinary ball but a touch less distance. At 38 grams, they weigh 3 grams less than regular balls. Their buoyancy is due to hollow, microscopic glass spheres within, and they float to the shore.

A water course.

Scuba divers trawl Stoneybrook's lakes for regular balls every month during the winter. Approximately 60,000 balls are retrieved annually; this equals the number of rounds played. Completing eighteen holes with the same ball is a major triumph. One scuba hound talked of the odd nip from a gator. How about crocodiles? "You wouldn't get me near the course if it had crocs," he replied. "Them critters are downright aggressive."

Hole one is rightly named the Omen. Water lies to the right off the tee, and cross bunkers stagger the fairway. The green has sand, trees, and a lake all behind. The second tee shot crosses water, bunkers pepper the right side of the fairway, and further left, pot bunkers will catch the longer hitter. The green complex is raised, with another bunker cluster to the left; the putting surface falls to the front right.

On paper the next five holes are easy, but we know what water does to paper. The third tempts a shot across the lake to the left side of the fairway; a tree hides a small depression with 150 yards to go. Sand sits to the left of the oval green. The fourth, despite being dubbed the Reprieve, has lakes at both sides of the tee box, with a ribbon bunker at the landing area. An approach shot might not hold, as the green's rear crown sheds balls left, right, and center. Five is Archipelago, and aptly named, a par 3 of 161 yards from an island tee to an island green surrounded by waste bunkers (see color plate 15).

Lone Oak is the sixth, and that solitary namesake stands 60 yards from the green. The putting surface drifts to the rear left from a central ridge. Another par 3 brings the "easy" section to a close. With 168 yards to the pin, the prevailing wind from the right should take the water and extensive bunkering out of the picture.

The eighth plays into the wind, its wide fairway narrowing from the 150-yard marker, while waste bunkers populated with a healthy spread of live oaks frame the left side. Nine is a forced carry over water to a wide fairway. Water then runs the length of the left side on this 546-yard par 5. As on three, a small depression sits in the fairway, marked by a live oak and a small palm. The fairway humps and bumps along, with bunkers narrowing the target. The two-tier green falls forward.

The tenth is a 516-yard par 5; the fairway flows between thin plantings of trees to an enormous green of 8,000 square feet. With around 4.5 acres of putting surface, most greens are on the large size and all are Tifdwarf, overseeded with *Poa trivialis* in winter. The fairways are GN-1, a hybrid Bermuda grass developed in Southern California; its dark green color and resilient properties have made it an established favorite for Superbowl and Olympic stadiums.

Number eleven plays along an avenue of slash pines with a sandy strand to the right housing a tree barrier. The thirteenth has a hidden waterhole in front of the green to the right. Keep left, going long off the tee. The target is well protected with sand fore and aft; the surface falls away to rear right.

At the fourteenth a 30-foot-wide band of turf connects the tee complex with the green. A collection bunker waits at front right on this par 3 of 213 yards. Fifteen requires a carry over water to a forgiving fairway bordered at left by a preservation area. The right runs with waste bunkers; a pot bunker sits left 100 yards from the wide, open green. A television announcer would pronounce this green unmissable.

Sixteen is a sweet hole, which doglegs over water. Gary Higgins, the course superintendent, has to aim over the trees to cut the corner. If he went for the fairway, he'd overshoot and end up in the lake. We're talking a drive of 280 yards. A handful of bunkers are placed greenside to catch players who have Gary's enviable problem.

The Final Drive is a par 5 with bunkering on both landing areas. The coquina-sand cart paths are considered waste bunkers, and you play your ball as you find it. Their shape is a welcome change from the typical concrete path urbanizing what should be greensward.

Part IV

Atlantic Coast to Key West

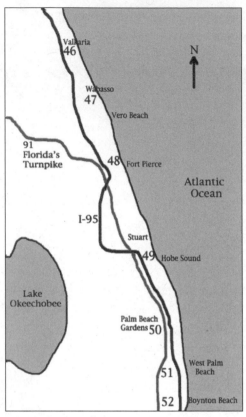

Atlantic Coast, Melbourne to Boynton Beach

46 The Habitat
47 Sandridge
48 Fairwinds
49 The Champions at Summerfield
50 PGA National
51 Okeeheelee
52 The Links at Boynton Beach

The Habitat at Valkaria

3591 Fairgreen Street, Valkaria 32950
(321) 952-6312
www.golfspacecoast.com

Green fee: $47

Architect: Charles Ankrom, 1991
Par 72
Blue yardage 6,074; course rating 69.9; slope rating 133
Green yardage 4,969; course rating 70.0; slope rating 119

Directions: From I-95 exit 173, take 514 (Malabar Road) east 0.5 miles. At 507
(Babcock Street), turn right (south) and go 3.1 miles to Valkaria Road. Turn
left (east); entrance (Fairgreen Street) is in 3.5 miles, on right.

A former World War II naval base was taken over by Brevard County to provide a buffer zone between the small airport and planned housing. Luckily for golf, the housing never materialized in force, and land abutting the course is now property of the Environmentally Endangered Lands program. Sighs of relief all around, as there's no chance for future development.

The course was laid out and built swiftly in 1991—the fairways were cleared in March and the course opened in October. Tifway 419 Bermuda grass is the fairway standard for this part of the world. The turf used for greens is another mainstay, Tifdwarf. On greens in the Frozen North, problems arise with fungus, but here in the blessed South it's bugs. Nematodes and mole crickets eat away at the grass root system, so annual application and constant supervision are necessary. Fire ants also do damage, and not just to the ground; at another course a superintendent dragged me from a nest where I stood perilously close.

The Habitat lies at the northern end of the sand ridge that runs south to West Palm Beach. Ten thousand years ago these were the seaside dunes of Florida, real old links land. In the 2004 hurricanes, a hundred trees were lost and 250 tons of sand had to be replaced. At $180 per ton, this is a significant cost.

Averaging about 100 rounds per day, the course is not crowded. Many courses look to 200 players, and some manage 250 daily. For this reason, the Habitat is allied with others in the region to benefit from shared advertising for stay-and-play packages. My advice is to visit before the marketing proves too successful.

The outward nine winds through pine forest. The 477-yard opener requires a hefty tee shot. Elevated bunkers guard the green on this left elbow. On number two, the right-hand side of the undulating fairway sets up good position to hit the target. A mid-iron approach to the green must avoid a deep bunker on the right.

Feel a touch of Kiawah Island at the third, a par 3 with a carry of 134 yards over water and a greenside bunker. The flip-chart guide on the cart reads: "Get out of here with a par and be happy."

The fourth is rated hardest hole, 386 yards angling right. A cloverleaf bunker, punctuated by a grass bullet, lies left of the small green. Another one-shot of 154 yards follows, but wind from behind can affect club selection. Aim left from the tee and fade in to the target. A three-bay bunker, shaped like a paw print, threatens to catch any slice.

Number four.

Nine's approach.

The next is a short par 4 along a corridor framed by sand pines, and the fairway is strewn with moguls. The second shot will likely be from an uphill or downhill lie. The green has a rear-left-to-front-right bias and is unprotected.

Water comes into play on the last three holes of this side. At the 365-yard seventh, if attempting greatness, try hitting from the 415-yard black tees. It's a long carry to a small landing area. The green is quite shallow and accessed most easily from the left. The eighth is a 474-yard par 5 to be treated with respect. Recreational golfers should lay up with their second and hit a wedge to the forward-sloping target. Big boys, no doubt, will choose driver and then 7-iron.

Divot holes in the fairway indicate the smart play on the ninth, leaving a 125-yard carry over water to an elevated green backed by pines. If the resident gator isn't coming at you, the chances are the wind will be. The alligator is one of a pair. The other is three-legged, the loser in the hardest-fought match play event ever at the Habitat.

Course manager and professional Alex Romanoff guided me around the more challenging back nine. The tenth's tee shot is into the wind to a thin landing area. Advice for the cautious is to lay up to the left and bump and run in to avoid bunkers left and right.

Frightening water makes a penal carry on the 177-yard par-3 eleventh, which favors a draw into an angled green. At least architect Ankrom was kind enough to omit sand hazards around this green. The next tee shot had me contemplating donning a skirt and lipstick to head for the forward tees; the forced carry over wetland must eat up balls by the dozen every day. From the 150-yard marker, a leaning live oak covers the left approach to the pancake green.

Depending on mindset, the final three holes crown the round or ruin the card. On a short par 4 at sixteen, the simple green gives no excuse for three putts. On seventeen I had to double-check the yardage—it looks longer than 142 yards. Perhaps the forced carry over a wide expanse of scrub gives this illusion. The 492-yard eighteenth is pure strategy. The first landing area is 25 yards wide and 75 yards long, and lies to the right of water and a waste bunker. You're now faced with a carry over water to a similar-sized fairway. If accurate enough with a 40-yard pitch to the tiny green, you're looking at birdie.

Other birdies visible on the way around include little blue herons, ibis, and scrub jays. You'll find a no-frills clubhouse and, quite frankly, fancy wouldn't suit here. This place is about the golf, the course, the wildlife and scenery—the habitat, naturally.

Sandridge Golf Club

5300 73rd Street, Vero Beach 32967
(561) 770-5000
www.sandridgegc.com

Green fee: $46

Architect: Ron Garl, 1987

Dunes		Lakes
72	Par	72
Blue/Red	Tees	Blue/Red
6,079/4,944	Yardage	5,856/4,625
70.7/69.3	Course rating	68.8/67.1
124/120	Slope rating	126/112

Directions: From I-95 exit 147, take 60 (20th Avenue) east 4.3 miles. At 58th Avenue turn left (north) and go 6.1 miles; entrance is on right.

From US 1 at Wabasso take 510 (Wabasso Road) west 0.6 miles. At 58th Avenue turn left (south) and go 1.5 miles; entrance is on left.

Chris Eckart, course superintendent at Sandridge, oversees thirty-six holes, a driving range, separate putting and chipping greens, cart paths, and all the vegetation comprising two courses, Dunes and Lakes. Most of the trees at Sandridge are slash pines, but pepper trees, a South American import, are a pest. In August 2004 controlled burning was conducted to weed out the unwanted inhabitants. Chris estimated a loss of 20 percent of the slash pines, but wasn't overly concerned. He wasn't expecting the events of September, however. The club was slammed by two hurricanes three weeks apart. The slash pines, still recovering from the burning, were stressed further, and hundreds of trees were lost. Four months later a newcomer would not know the difference; both courses looked in superb shape.

Six acres of greens are overseeded annually in November. With 250 rounds played daily in winter, the dormant Bermuda dwarf grass needs help. A combination of perennial rye and *Poa trivialis* grow in, but burn off in the heat of the summer. Players go off the first tee and the tenth tee simultaneously for

Daunting tee shot on Dunes number four.

two hours in the morning and again at lunchtime. At a private club this doesn't happen. The superintendent can send out one mower before the first foursome of the day and greens can be cut and pin placements adjusted without interfering with, or interference from, the players. Chris has to treat Sandridge as if he had four nine-hole courses, thus sending out four mowers ahead of play. He has a staff of twenty-one, including two assistants and two mechanics. Regular eighteen-hole courses usually have one mechanic and an assistant.

I suggested he must breathe a sigh of relief on May first when the winter traffic has gone. Not really, he replied; that's when he shuts down one course for radical aeration. A two-week vacation has it restored to condition. The other course then undergoes the same treatment.

His computerized water sprinkler system has no schedule. "You can't regularize when you water," he said. "There are variables to consider, such as evapo-transpiration factors." I nodded inanely. Grass root systems, known as thatch, must be kept to an optimum thickness, a bit like fat on a body—in the case of greens, 1.0 to 1.5 inches. Verticutting gives the green the appearance of having been attacked with a circular saw; in fact, it's a remedial thinning of the subcutaneous thatch.

The Dunes course is built upon the site of a sand mine with natural lakes and large, native waste areas. It has excellent drainage but is handled more gently with regard to fertilizer, which disappears rapidly. Conversely, Lakes is on heavier soil and has drainage problems but can withstand large applications of fertilizer. Sand in time gets blown away, so bunkers are replenished every other year to a minimum of three inches.

With all this attention to a frail ecosystem, a sensitive soul would think twice before playing golf here. Please don't hesitate; both courses are wonderful tracks with beautiful scenery, and away from houses. Just consider what goes into the preparation of a golf course for your enjoyment. And while you're repairing your own pitch mark, have a heart and do another couple as well.

Dunes is the favorite son of the two courses here. An easy opener is a gift from course architect Ron Garl, who shows his teeth at the par-5 second. This does no favors for the long hitter wanting to get home in two. A lake runs along the fairway from 175 yards out and shields the front of the green. Three is a pretty one-shot hole given height and depth by tall slash pines on the right and at the rear. Wading birds stoop mournfully as if looking for balls sucked into the lake on the left.

The most daunting tee shot on Dunes is the fourth—a carry over a strip of fairway pinched by water on both sides. The hole doglegs right with 180 yards remaining. Sandy waste lines the right side. The green is a small target of 2,200 square feet. The sixth hops 131 yards across water to a peninsular green. Holes eight and nine are reminiscent of English heathland courses such as Sunning-dale, with thin undulating runways funneled by tall trees.

The back nine is where Dunes really comes into its own. The opening holes play out to the old sand mine. Twelve doglegs 450 yards around a vast waste area and water. The thirteenth uses camouflage in abundance. From a blind tee shot, a waste area crosses the right and a bunker planted with cordgrass lies left. With 150 yards to go, a cross hazard is invisible in a depression 40 yards before the green.

The 153 yard seventeenth plays uphill across a lake. The green, sloping from rear right to front left, favors a high fade. Take a longer club than normal at this distance and, if playing in springtime when windy, maybe two clubs longer. So generous to start off with an easy hole, Ron Garl is not so sympathetic on the return home. Sand slices across the fairway to catch the 300-yard-plus drive. Low handicappers can reach the green in two; for the rest of us it's a three-shot play.

The Lakes course's back nine shares ground with the Dunes front nine. Fourteen is a 388-yard dogleg left, playing into an island green. The 472-yard fourth is most spectacular. Three bunkers swallow anything left of the landing

Lakes shares ground with Dunes front nine.

area; clearing them leaves the better approach to the green. If short and right of the pin, the player is amid a cluster of pot bunkers, and hitting to an elevated target.

Sandridge regulars have their own secret course. When asked their preference, all replied, "Back nine Dunes and front nine Lakes."

Fairwinds Golf Course

4400 Fairwinds Drive, Fort Pierce 34946
(772) 462-1955
www.stlucieco.gov/fairwinds

Green fee: $42

Architect: Jim Fazio, 1991
Par 72
Blue yardage 6,211; course rating 69.2; slope rating 118
Gold yardage 4,994; course rating 68.5; slope rating 113

*Directions: From I-95 North exit 131, go east on 68 (Orange Avenue) 4.2 miles.
At US 1 turn left (north), go 4.4 miles, and turn in to Fairwinds Drive on the
left; entrance to the club is 0.3 miles ahead.*

*From I-95 South exit 138, go east on 614 east (Indrio Road) 5.8 miles. At US
1 turn right (south), go 1.2 miles, and turn in to Fairwinds Drive on the right;
entrance to the club is 0.3 miles ahead.*

Fairwinds Golf Course is a delightful story of garbage turned into gold. Me-
dieval alchemists would have sold their souls for such transformation. A winner in Best Places to Play surveys on local and national levels, Fairwinds was
beaten by Pebble Beach by only half a star in one popular rating. The course,
owned and operated by St. Lucie County, was built upon the county's former
landfill. For years it was strictly for the birds and scavengers to sort through.
The landfill closed, and the idea for a golf course was raised.

Jim Fazio's design incorporates rolling elevation changes to allow variety in
the shape of the holes and in the shots needed to complete them. Although the
slope rating designates it a relatively easy course, there are a couple of tee shots
to set the adrenaline pumping. Hit and hang on to your hat. Fairwinds could
more aptly be called Wildwinds; the sou'easter is a constant in winter.

This course has been so busy from day one that in early 2005 they were turning away a hundred players every day. Another eighteen holes under construction on adjacent land to the north should be up and running for the 2006–7
season.

An easy away at the first leads to two of the most difficult holes. The second is straight and wide, the approach into a two-tier green sloping from rear right to front left. Bunkers are placed at these corners. The greens at Fairwinds tend to follow this slope pattern. The 416-yard third has mounded bunkers along the left side of the fairway and a deep greenside bunker to the right.

The par-5 fourth faces into the prevailing wind, feeling longer than its recorded 497 yards. Scrub lines the right side, and two pot bunkers sit 50 yards before the green. A massive bunker is buried greenside right. This is the third consecutive green to slope from rear right to front left.

Five, the first and longest of the par 3s, has the player hitting into the wind. The green is hipped by a three-bay bunker at left and two pots to the right. At least the next, another par 5, gives wind advantage.

The seventh doglegs right, with attractive bunkering on both sides giving the fairway a frayed look. At the 100-yard marker it curves sharply right and downhill to a flat green. The second par 3 plays 185 yards, and again into the wind. The putting surface has a rear-right-to-front-left bias once more. The front nine ends with a 250-yard drive into a valley fairway. Clearing the sand hazard at the landing area leaves a 150-yard approach.

Into the prevailing wind.

The back nine winds around a lake system, a touch shorter than the outward but a shade more difficult. On ten, water is in play down the right-hand side, scrub lines the left, and the left-sloping green is guarded in front by a pot bunker. The eleventh is only 118 yards, and uphill. The angled green has no obvious traps, though sloping forward and backward from a central ridge, where it is no more than nine yards wide.

What should be a workaday par four of 327 yards on twelve precedes one of my favorites at Fairwinds. A par 5, thirteen doglegs right around a lake. A chain of aiming bunkers links the outer angle for those playing safe. Big hitters should aim across the lake to the trees, leaving a long-iron approach. The fairway is 25–28 yards wide at this point, giving plenty of room to land. The elevated green, however, is well guarded all around. On a naturalist note, this area is preserved habitat for the Florida scrub jay, one of the state's most endangered species. Predominantly blue in color, with a white throat and breast, it is distinguishable from the blue jay by having a dark patch around the eye and a brown mantle.

The round delivers a rousing finish. The frightening tee shot at fifteen (see color plate 16) is a breeze if you can whack the ball 250 yards. With the wind at your back and a solid connection, the ball will soar over the water, clear a large paw-print bunker, land between two thin stands of trees, and roll downhill to the 150-yard marker. The two-tier green has a ridge at center left dispersing balls to the right.

The 354-yard sixteenth is a handsome left-to-right hole. Bunkers and mounds define the angle leading downhill to the undulating green; a bunker draped from greenside left is the only protection.

On the par-5 seventeenth, the bench-terrace green is cut into a steep bank, which falls away to the left. Approaching from the high right risks landing in an elevated bunker. Too hefty from the sand means the next shot will be played from way below the green.

The home tee sits on the highest part of the old landfill where all the old washing machines and dryers were buried. The tee shot plays to a neck of land with water at both sides. Common sense dictates the green must be near the clubhouse, but it is hard to make out from the tee. The fairway veers left from the landing area to a shallow putting surface with water and sand to the right.

Course superintendent Christopher Gamble told me the landfill was the trench-and-fill type, with which we are all familiar, I'm sure. Occasionally some refuse works its way to the surface. When the lakes are low, the odd tire will appear. The main intruders, though, are feral pigs that eat up the fairways; at least they have the decency to leave tees and greens alone.

The Champions Club at Summerfield

3400 SE Summerfield Way, Stuart 34997
(772) 283-1500
www.championsclubsummerfield.com

Green fee: $65

Architect: Tom Fazio, 1995
Par 72
Blue yardage 6,335; course rating 70.8; slope rating 126
Green yardage 4,941; course rating 69.2; slope rating 117

Directions: From I-95 exit 101, take 76 east for 0.6 miles. At Cove Road turn right and go 3.1 miles to US 1. Turn right (south); entrance is on right in 0.8 miles.

While researching Florida's golf courses, I visited a particular venue in a beautiful community with a great golf course design and variation in housing to attract families, seniors, and second-home owners. After I completed my hole-by-hole analysis and took my photographs, the management proudly announced they were soon to turn private. I made my sad exit, driving the mile along a soon-to-be-private road parallel to the perimeter holes. The community had no gates as yet, but I knew the next time I went by, there would be barriers and a security guard. What an indictment of human society that we have to construct fortress communities in which to feel safe. I was getting too philosophical at this point and pulled into a gateless community I was assured welcomed members of the general public.

Golf Magazine named the Champions Club at Summerfield among the nation's Top Ten New Public Courses upon opening in 1995. It also holds the distinction of being the first public course to be awarded Audubon Signature Sanctuary status. In 2002 the National Junior Championship was held here.

The golf winds through marshy wetlands, and while houses are visible from a couple of fairways, they are not intrusive. Rustic wooden boardwalks run from green to tee and the place is rich with wildlife.

Rustic boardwalks
cross the wetlands.

Tom Fazio supplies a quick getaway with a straight par 4 between tall pines. The small green has a bunker at the rear. A par 3 follows with a forced carry over a swamp. The putting surface tilts left. The third is a playful dogleg right. Wetland forces carry off the tee. A tree to the right looks closer to the green than the bunkers to the left; in fact, they are the better line. A 250-yard fade should roll to mid-iron range. A pair of sandhill cranes patrolled the landing area, alert as forecaddies.

Sometimes danger is dressed in the prettiest packaging. The 115-yard sixth is played over swamp to a green with bunkers as elaborate as carnival costumes. Hole seven has trouble the whole length on the left side, from wetland that

Homes set back from the tenth fairway.

digs into the fairway to the bunker at the front of the green. It's all set up for a back-left pin placement.

On the eighth, aim for the left fairway bunker; 100 yards of bog will collect flunked tee shots all day. A two-tiered green falls away to the rear and is ringed by bunkers.

Nine is a par 4 of 363 yards. Attached to the cart is a hole-by-hole flip chart of laminated pages thick as placemats. I mused, awkwardly turning the leaves of this plastic manual, a remnant of on-cart guidance systems in their infancy: With GPS on carts and personal GPS devices on the market, have we conquered the numbers game? The future could bring such precise exchanges as:

"Well, I was at 691241 this morning and went into a bunker."

"That bunker at 691241? I know that one! Near the water to the left of 693237?"

"Yes, that's right. How did your game go at 712819 last weekend, by the way?"

"Absolute stinker, I'm sorry to say. Went into the 714727 behind the 713724, and took five to get out!"

The far left corner of the fairway leaves the easiest approach over wetland to a modest-sized green. I gave myself two putts here as the sky opened with a flash of lightning and rumbles of thunder and rain came pouring down. A frustrated fleet of carts scurried back to the clubhouse, our rounds scuttled for the day. I am pleased to note everybody was given a rain check.

The forward tees differ from the back by an average of 100 yards. Choose the set appropriate for your ability; there's little point in playing a course "from the tips" just to cover every square inch. To disprove my theory, Bob, a homeowner here, finds it safer to play from the longer tees. "On this course the landing area for a 230-yard drive is narrower from the whites than the blues. So it's a simple choice—I play from the blues." Bob grew up in Bethpage, New York, and caddied there as a youngster. I saw no reason to doubt his course management. His house here is far from the playing area. "I don't want to be woken up at six-thirty every morning by the mowing crew," he said.

The eleventh is the only hole hemmed in by housing on three sides. A bunkered fairway mound gives the nod to play left, leaving a wedge to a large two-tiered green. The one-shot twelfth plays 194 yards with trouble on the left all the way. A distorted cloverleaf bunker sits right of the two-tier green, displaying the same high-left bias as the previous hole.

Two easy par 4s give a breather before a strong finish. Fourteen has the narrower fairway of the pair, but its green is unguarded. Fifteen has a more receptive landing area with strategically placed sand for approaches wide and short. The sixteenth has lost a little grace with the building of houses to the left of the fairway. Otherwise, it's a 398-yard par 4 with a forward-sloping green.

Seventeen is an attractive one-shot hole with plenty of sand to the left of a green slanted, as is the trend here, from the rear left quarter. The home hole is a par 5, where water accepts any push or slice in the final 250 yards. A center-parted green invites a choice of sand hazard: one long and shallow to the right, or two deep to the left. The long cart ride to the clubhouse provides passengers with a perfect opportunity to add up their scores—or double-check their opponents'.

PGA National Golf Club

1000 Avenue of Champions, Palm Beach Gardens 33418
(561) 627-1800
www.pgaresort.com

	The Champion	The Haig	The General
Green Fee	$270	$208	$208
(Rack rates, for resorts guests only. Packages are available.)			
Architect	Jack Nicklaus	Tom Fazio	Arnold Palmer
Year	1990	1980	1984
Par	72	72	72
Tees	Blue/Red	Blue/Red	Blue/Red
Yardage	6,379/5,145	6,806/5,645	6,768/5,327
Course rating	71.6/72.3	73.5/73.6	73.1/71.9
Slope rating	137/136	139/135	134/125

Directions: From I-95 exit 79, go west on 786 (PGA Boulevard) 2.2 miles; entrance is on left.

From 91 (Florida's Turnpike) exit 109, go west on 786 (PGA Boulevard) 0.4 miles; entrance is on left.

Southeast Florida's supreme golf resort is first class from the moment one enters the property. Guests have five courses to choose from. The Haig is the oldest, the Champion the most prestigious; the General, the Squire, and the Estate complete the picture.

The Champion has to be included in the money-no-object category. It hosted the Ryder Cup in 1983, the PGA Championship in 1987, and a decade of Senior PGA Championships, as well as PGA Junior and PGA Cup Team Matches. The 1981 Tom Fazio design was remodeled in 1990 by Jack Nicklaus and his team. Another update in 2002 served to renew irrigation and drainage systems. From 2007, it will be the venue for the PGA Tour Honda Classic.

Five sets of tees leave plenty of scope for golfers of varied abilities, affording a pleasant round for some to say they've "been there," yet challenging enough for others to say they've "done that." Set off in the morning with the sun at your back down the first. From an elevated tee the fairway rides down to a green in

Fifteen, start of
the three-hole
Bear Trap.

a handsome setting. The par-5 third doglegs left with a bunker to the right of
the target. A small flight of wooden steps leads into the sand, indicating no easy
recovery. A short par 4 is next. Two deep bunkers cover the left fairway at the
150-yard marker. The greenside bunker to the right also has those steps!

The fifth measures 138 yards to a large green fronted by water. No problem,
you think, take one more club . . . careful here, the wind is usually from your
back, and a trap runs behind the target from left to center. Number six is a su-
per par 5; bunkers flow along the right-hand side as water does opposite. The
heart-shaped green, only half as wide as it is deep, gives entry from the right.

Seven is the longer of this side's par 3s and calls for a draw over heavy bunkering.

I wondered why the eighth, a short par 4, is stroke index 2 when, reaching the landing area, I discovered a lake lying between my ball and the green, which is raised and flanked by sand on both sides. My attention wandered to the cormorants, storks, and pelicans, none of which seemed to mind being in the water at all.

A strong finish to the front side requires a tee shot over water. The fairway doglegs left to an elevated green faced by a trap as deep as a quarry. Two more conventional hazards guard the right and rear.

The back nine begins with a simple par 5 that plays downhill to a broad fairway and a small green with some sand. The eleventh, by contrast, is rated hardest hole. This 395-yard par 4 is flanked by water from the 150-yard marker and floods the approach to the green. The putting surface slopes away from the front left quarter; a deep pot bunker waits behind for those who strive too hard clearing the pond.

A stone marker warns you have just entered the Bear Trap. Fifteen, sixteen, and seventeen are considered a tough combination. The 153-yard one-shot features an all-water carry. Sixteen doglegs sharply right. From the angle 200 yards remain, with a carry over water. Bunkers lie beneath the green to the right. The Sunday pin placement is back left, and everything falls away from this high point.

Seventeen's tees form a semicircle around a lake, with water forcing carry for the third hole in a row. Play is into the prevailing wind, and a yawning bunker waits behind the forward-sloping green. The pressure is kept up at the 527-yard eighteenth, again with water in play. The fairway is bunkered at both sides in the landing zone. Pot bunkers line the left side of the approach; the lake covers the right. Bunkers and an amphitheater of mounding surround the green, a champion finish to the Champion—the wonder course.

The Haig is named for golf's flamboyant showman, Walter Hagen. Rose bushes bloom on each hole at the 150-yard marker, honoring his reminder to "stop and smell the roses." The first is a par-5 double dogleg to a small green. The next six holes play around a circle of houses. After two innocuous par 4s, the fourth taxes wits, strength, and stamina over 566 yards. Bunkers lie in slice range from the tee, on the second shot, and at greenside.

The headquarters of the PGA of America provides a backdrop to the fifth green; the building's International style is reminiscent of Hagen's heyday. Houses to the left of the eighth tee have neo-mansard roofing; italianate towers and tiled roofs stand over to the right. I'm sure most players are gazing at the thin, rolling fairway rather than the architecture. Two mounded bunkers to the right leave blind the 50 yards between their position and the green.

The close of the Haig contains four of its most difficult holes. Left of the wide landing area is favored on fourteen; the green is bunkered left and right. Fifteen is a dogleg right and just out of driving range even for the gripping, ripping gorilla-type player. The small green is bunkered on all sides (see color plate 17). The sixteenth, a 210-yard par 3, shares a lake with the previous hole. The forward-sloping green also tilts from right to left, where a sand hazard gathers those shots neither high nor long enough to reach this elevated table.

A light aircraft could land on the seventeenth fairway, it is so long. From 200 yards away you cannot see the water by the target. At 150 yards you imagine merely a small pond to the left. With a wedge in hand at 100 yards, it is evident the lake curls all the way in front of the fortress green, guarded by bunkers at the rear. The home hole twists to the right with a trio of sand hazards at the apex. Water runs all along the left to a tight little green buttressed by bunkers.

On the General, Arnold Palmer's design plays out to the tenth, then turns back on itself all the way home. This echoes the style of Scottish links courses such as Prestwick, Royal Troon, and St. Andrews. After the scenic opener, the testy third, and the lengthy fourth, the middle section is quite forgiving. The crunch comes from the fifteenth onward, and the holes keep getting longer. The 567-yard finisher will have you hoping those aren't the final three numbers on your card.

Okeeheelee Golf Course

1200 Country Club Way, West Palm Beach 33413
(561) 964-4653
www.okeeheeleegolf.com

Green fee: $55

Architect: Roy Case, 1995

Gold/White	Eagle+Osprey	Osprey+Heron	Heron+Eagle
Par	72	72	72
Yardage	6,267/5,257	6,393/5,398	6,556/5,453
Course rating	69.9/70.7	70.5/72.0	71.0/72.3
Slope rating	124/115	· 122/116	122/116

Directions: From I-95 exit 66, go west on 882 (Forest Hill Boulevard) 5.6 miles. At the junction with Pinehurst Drive, entrance is on right.

From 91 Florida Turnpike exit 93, go east on 802 (Lake Worth Road) 1 mile. At Pinehurst Drive turn left (north) and go 2.3 miles; entrance faces across Forest Hill Boulevard.

Okeeheelee is a success story for Palm Beach County. The county's first involvement in running a golf facility arose when it acquired 1,200 acres of land previously worked as a sand mine and transformed them into a park and recreational facility. In planning a nature center, football, baseball, and soccer fields, and biking and rambling trails, 200 acres were set aside for golf. Golf course architect Roy Case was enlisted to design twenty-seven holes with absolutely no housing.

Private clubs have greater leeway with irrigation; public facilities are more accountable when it comes to water sources and disposal. As all architects and superintendents will tell you, the three most important elements of golf course design are drainage, drainage, and drainage. One regulation denied use of the central lake, a feature on Heron and Eagle, for irrigation or disposal, so other ponds were included to do the work (see color plate 18).

Stephen Cox, Okeeheelee's general manager and director of golf, explained how tee times are managed at a 27-hole public course. A nine-hole course is easy to operate: send people out and they come back. Eighteen holes give the option of sending players out from the first and tenth simultaneously, as on the first two days of a professional tournament. Inevitably, the 7:00 a.m. tenth-tee group will be coming to start their back nine around 9:00 a.m., the group behind them at 9:06, the next at 9:12, and so on until about 11:00 a.m., when everyone who started at 7:00 a.m. has finished. (Are you following me? Please keep up.) Apply this to Okeeheelee: Eagle goes to Osprey, Osprey goes to Heron, and Heron goes to Eagle. Which is why last-minute callers can't get a start time between 9:30 and noon. The afternoon is similarly staggered. Fortunately, there are no memberships to tie up tee times, but advance booking is advised.

The three nines begin in like fashion with a par 5 followed by a par 3. This gets three groups away on the first hole—one putting out, the second on the fairway, and the third on the tee. The par 3 takes up the pace and establishes a rhythm for the round. Eagle and Osprey fold around each other for these first two holes, with doglegs left for openers and attractive one-shots played to greens backed by stands of tall gumbo-limbo trees. All trees are implants; it's amazing how hardy some can be on a combination of shell rock and sugar sand.

View from Osprey's fourth tee.

Eagle's third has fairway bunkers but an unprotected green. Four has an empty fairway but two greenside hazards. How many golfers will appreciate this intentional ebb and flow? From the blue tee, hole five floats uphill 340 yards, while six glides downhill two yards shorter. The par-3 seventh has the green's entrance blocked by an optical mound; the flag is visible, but little else. The finishing holes grab players by the collar if they are getting away with a good score. Eight is a 473-yard dogleg left to a green that was once tiny but is now just on the small side. The finisher fades around Okeeheelee's central lake, with bunkers to the left and rear of the green.

Heron is the hardest of the nines. It plays out and back in a loop, only the middle holes paralleling each other. To begin, the longest par 5 goes doglegging to the edge of the property. Perimeter trees line the left-hand side of the next two. Three's green has a bunker to the right, four has one to the left, and five has a horseshoe bunker all the way around the rear—design variation and symmetry the purist will appreciate.

The sixth is my candidate for the toughest at this venue. Fairway hazards narrow the landing area off the tee, water runs to the left, and a large bunker sits greenside left. Keep high and right is the duffer's advice. The final three holes have no bunkers at all. There are only thirty-seven bunkers serving twenty-seven holes, displaying the architect's opinion that a bunker is a hole in the ground into which money is continually poured.

On Heron's seventh, water must be crossed twice to get to home. Eight is played to an elevated green; most players come up short on what looks an easy 362 yards. From the black tees, the ninth rises to a green 209 yards distant; the forward tees, however, hit down into the target.

A beautiful view it is from Osprey's fourth tee in the early morning, looking across the land and water it shares with Eagle. Okeeheelee means "quiet waters" in the language of the Seminole. From the fifth until completion Osprey winds within the core of Heron's nine. Numbers five and six are fraternal twins to Heron's one and two. The kick in the pants comes at Osprey's ninth, the hardest hole. Initially intended as a par 4, it was extended to make par equal 36. You drive north, then wedge west, so you can head north again. Not unlike driving in Florida.

With 90,000 rounds of golf per year, it's a testament to the designer and management that Okeeheelee remains a public facility worthy of plaudits. The county has taken to the golf business like a duck to water. Another two courses, one of twenty-seven holes, are due to open in 2006.

Heron and Eagle garnered most votes among the staff and volunteers as the favored eighteen-hole combination, although visually my preference is Osprey. At Okeeheelee I met a man who enjoys Osprey so much he played it twice in one afternoon. Mind you, what does he know? He only designed the place.

The Links at Boynton Beach

8020 Jog Road, Boynton Beach 33437
(561) 742-6501
www.boynton-beach.org

Green Fees: $49

Architects: Robert von Hagge, Bruce Devlin, and Charles Ankrom, 1984
Par 71
Gold yardage 6,297; course rating 68.0; slope rating 123
Red yardage 4,739; course rating 67.2; slope rating 111

*Directions: From I-95 exit 57, go west on 804 (Boynton Beach Boulevard) 4.6
miles. At Jog Road turn right (north); in 2.0 miles, entrance is on right.*

*From 91 (Florida's Turnpike) exit 86, go east on 804 (Boynton Beach Boule-
vard) 1.5 miles. At Jog Road, turn left (north); in 2.0 miles, entrance is on right.*

Head golf professional Dan Hager is one of the nicest men you'll ever meet.
When he's not serving as state divisional director of the Salvation Army, he's
honing the operations at Boynton Beach. He conducts gap surveys to find out
what his golfers want. Humor is one of his tools. A sign by the roadside entrance reads "Public Only."

There are some members of the public he doesn't encourage, the slow ones.
A well-publicized incident involved a couple who, after repeated requests to
pick up their pace, were ejected from the course for slow play. They complained
to the highest authorities. Rather than reprimanding Dan, the USGA and the
Royal and Ancient Golf Club applauded his action.

This reminds us, one obligation as players is to keep up with the group
ahead, not just ahead of the group behind. It is symptomatic of the times that
a round is taking four-hours-plus. Three and a half is considered the norm in
the auld country. Perhaps too much television or too much aspiration is making amateurs assume the meticulousness of golfers on the professional tours.
Lighten up, general public, these guys and gals are indeed good and they are
playing for a living. We are doing it for fun, aren't we?

If you were to present Florida Municipal Golf gift-wrapped, it would look
something like Boynton Beach, a core course within a rectangle. The front nine

The fifteenth.

occupies the southeast half, with holes running north and south. The back nine plays west and east in the northwest half. The land is essentially flat, but humps and hollows introduce variety. Water and sand share billing as hazards. To find so much birdlife within such a compact area adds to the attraction.

A 509-yard opener with bunkers on the right welcomes slices short and long. The fairway elbows left at wedge distance to a small green. Anything too long or left will end up in water. The second hole, a par 3, faces into the prevailing wind, so club up accordingly. Australian pines line the right side of the fairway and shield the canal beyond. Bunkers cover the left entrance of a forward-sloping green. Three too has a canal framing its right-hand side, but plenty of room to the left gives easier access to the target.

At the fifth, a 50-yard pitch would carry the water sitting immediately off the tee; why then is water so intimidating with a 3-wood in my hands? Aim at the ribbon fairway bunker. Placement as far left as possible avoids crossing a nasty pot bunker crouching at the mouth of the green. Its whiskery edge winks at traditional links bunkers.

Water comes into play on the next three holes. The rough is kept a little longer close to water hazards to prevent chemical seepage. Here, organic sprays and natural fertilizers are preferred treatments; chemicals are used as a last resort. The sixth doglegs right over 358 yards, and a lake covers the left approach fringing the front of the green. Slope drags everything to the rear left quarter; an enthusiastic draw will roll into the drink. The seventh is a par 3 of 186 yards. Water on the left steers many to push right, where sits a yawning greenside bunker.

Eight is a tantalizingly short par 4 measuring 307 yards. The lake, hidden from the tee by a mounded fairway bunker, almost isolates the green. The ninth fairway has an aiming bunker at 250 yards from the tee and 75 yards from the green, which is cornered by sand.

Oriental orchid trees stand by the tenth where a straight par 4 continues the round. This stretch proves a little longer and more competitive. The view from the eleventh tee on my last visit was a forest of pines behind aiming bunkers. These hazards sit at the outer angle of a ninety-degree dogleg to the right, 515 yards in length and rated hardest hole at Boynton Beach. Twelve emulates eleven in formation and difficulty, a right-angled fairway with a beautiful setting. The tee shot plays toward a backdrop of two large bunkers, which are set in a slope against a perimeter pine stand. Azaleas would bring replica status.

Sixteen doglegs left 386 yards, with a long carry over water from the tee. The hole is sandwiched between two par 3s. Fifteen skirts water all the way along the left; the seventeenth is more penal, with water in front and right of the target.

The club motto is "Growing the Game and Our People," meaning not only members and visitors but also staff and local residents. Children receive a background in golf history and etiquette as well as how to swing a club. A recent program incorporates autistic students from the neighboring Park Vista High School into the grounds staff. The venue hosts the South Florida Senior/Junior Pro-Pro Championship and a sectional qualifier for the Women's Amateur Public Links Championship.

To promote the friendly and nurturing atmosphere, a nine-hole, par-30 Family Course has three par 4s and contains a picturesque trio played around a lake. Five sets of tees accommodate players from the scratch to the scratchy.

Blue herons, cormorants, anhingas, and iguanas are neighbors; a couple of shy alligators too are resident. Everybody gets on with each other at the Links at Boynton Beach. It's about community.

A backdrop of pines on eleven.

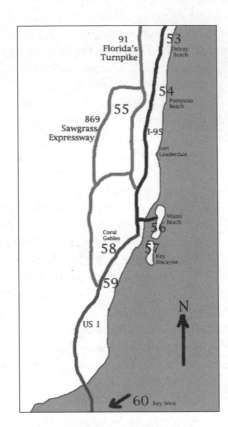

Delray Beach to Miami
and Key West

53 Delray Beach
54 Pompano Beach
55 Colony West
56 Miami Beach
57 Crandon
58 The Biltmore
59 Palmetto
60 Key West

Delray Beach Golf Club

2200 Highland Avenue, Delray Beach 33445
(561) 243-7380
www.jcdsportsgroup.com/delray_beach_golf_club

Green fee: $55

Architect: Donald Ross, 1923
Par 72
Blue yardage 6,360; course rating 69.9; slope rating 111
White yardage 5,189; course rating 68.4; slope rating 111

Directions: From I-95 exit 52, take 806 (Atlantic Avenue) west 0.8 miles to Homewood Boulevard. Turn left, go 0.5 miles to Highland Avenue, and turn left again; entrance is ahead.

From 91 (Florida's Turnpike) exit 81, take 806 (Atlantic Avenue) east 4.5 miles to Homewood Boulevard. Turn right, go 0.5 miles to Highland Avenue, and turn left; entrance is ahead.

Designed by Donald Ross in 1923, this club is drenched with history. If you've never played one of his courses before, this is a grand starter—unless you prefer to jump in at the deep end and try Pinehurst No. 2, site of Payne Stewart's memorable victory at the 1999 U.S. Open and that of New Zealander Michael Campbell six years later. Don't expect crown greens, though; those here are on the small side, and many slope forward. What you will find is sand, lots of it, everywhere. The terrain is typically flat, so the greens tend to be on raised pads. Most holes play straight, but six of them dogleg. The maturity of the trees is a constant reminder of the age of the course.

There is a strong tradition of ladies' golf at Delray Beach. My first visit coincided with the annual clinic given by Beth Daniel and Meg Mallon in January. In attendance was the great Betty Jameson, one of thirteen founders of the LPGA and golf's first glamour girl. She won fourteen titles as an amateur, including the 1932 Texas Publinks at the age of thirteen, and two U.S. Women's Amateur trophies. She beat a full field at the 1942 Western Open, in those days ranked as a major. Turning professional, she collected the U.S. Women's Open

Looking back to the tenth tee.

in 1947 with a score of 295, the first female player to break 300 for a 72-hole tournament. The Jameson Pro-Am is another calendar highlight at the club.

An official LPGA event, the Louise Suggs Invitational, was held here in 1966. Mickey Wright, who racked up four U.S. Women's Open titles among her 82 professional victories, once lived in a house next to the eighth fairway. The current director of instruction is Sandra Eriksson, 1999 LPGA Professional of the Year, who must be acknowledged as the source of historical content in this chapter.

Men are no wallflowers at Delray Beach. Sarazen, Snead, and Nelson all competed here. Tommy Armour taught here for fifteen years, instructing from beneath a parasol with drink in hand. Dick Wilson, designer of the Blue Course at Doral, was greenkeeper in the 1930s. After World War II some men of senior years started a thrice-weekly golfing group that became known as the Inner Circle, perhaps the first and certainly the longest-running senior golf association in the state. Some members never left the course, even after joining the Big Club. Wakes were held, and ashes scattered.

The first tee shot can set the tone of a round. With a small canal running along the right side of the first, we all hope that tone won't be a crack followed by a splash. A large spreading ficus leans its boughs over the bank as if trying to see its own reflection in the water. Bunkers guard both front quarters of the green. The second shapes left around a lake to another forward-sloped, front-bunkered green. I was told to club up on approach because of the elevation, always mindful of the dictum that hackers tend to come up short.

Four looks a monster from the tee box; two enormous bunkers dominate the left angle of the fairway. Ross tempts a draw to clear them and leave an easy second. Mere mortals should place their shots to the right and consider a layup on this 418-yard par 4. A pitch over greenside bunkers might end close enough to save par on Delray Beach's hardest hole.

The short par-4 fifth needs the ball threaded between a large bunker to the right of the fairway and four others cornering the pancake green. Hazards abound on the 162-yard sixth, the canal runs to the right, and there's no bailout area.

Eight's fairway bunker measures 28 yards in length and is placed 120 yards from the flag. My jaws opened wider with every new stretch of sand. By the green, two more sandy saucers resembled footprints of some enormous alien elephant.

A dogleg left ends the front side. Strong players will want to cut the corner (bunkered, of course), leaving 200 yards to a forward-sloping green. Sand hazards sit just shy of the target.

Sand, lots of sand.

The tenth has postcard views looking back to the clubhouse from 250 yards out, and forward to the green backed by a semicircle of royal palms. Bunkers pinch the entrance into a narrow funnel.

At eleven a dry lake forces a carry off the tee. Three pot bunkers line the fairway for fifty yards at the 150-yard marker. The twelfth is the monster on the back nine: 500 yards, with helpful signs by flashed bunkers indicating "200 yards to water" and "250 yards to carry water."

Thirteen is a daunting 188-yard one-shot. A bunker at left and others to the right and rear encircle the green. Fifteen, a 490-yard par 5, had me wondering how much bunkering can save on mowing costs.

Staring down the fairway from the sixteenth tee, I expected Lawrence of Arabia to appear any minute. Sand hazards lie to the left, the left, and the left again. To compound the effect, bunkers prop up both sides of the green.

At the par-3 seventeenth it's almost a relief to have to cross the canal first and THEN the front bunker. A rear bunker collects tee shots unable to hold 20 yards of green depth. The home hole is a simple finish, providing you avoid the sand on both sides of the landing area. A raised target sits to the right at fairway's end. A day at the beach indeed.

City of Pompano Beach Golf Course

1101 N Federal Highway, Pompano Beach 33062
(954) 786-4142

Green fee: $47.50

Architects: Bruce Devlin and Robert von Hagge, 1967

Pines		Palms
72	Par	72
Blue/Red	Tees	Blue/Red
6,598/5,530	Yardage	6,035/5,133
70.6/71.5	Course rating	68.6/64.3
116/123	Slope rating	111/102

Directions: From I-95 exit 38, go east on Copans Road 2.1 miles to US 1 and turn right (south); entrance is on right in 0.8 miles.

Once the busiest course in the nation, this 36-hole von Hagge and Devlin creation is a blue-collar classic. Two-time major winner Sandra Palmer won an LPGA event here in 1973, the Pompano Beach Classic. The two courses, Pines and Palms, interweave like the warp and weft of a garment, with Pines holding the outer hem, keeping everything from unraveling. Bordered on one perimeter by an executive airport and the other by US 1, you certainly know you're playing in a city. A few holes into the round, you're lost in trees, a mixture of palms and pines of course, savoring slowly the threads of fairway, taking the texture of humps and hillocks, guessing the gentle rub of the greens.

Golf has come a long way from an unattended trust box where you deposited your green fee to Pompano's racetrack cashier windows. It's strictly first come, first served: you show up, pay up, and then wait your turn. Old members remember when they used to line up the carts and go for breakfast.

Dennis, the starter, recalls when men wanted to play Pines, and Palms was considered for the ladies. All is changed since a facelift at the turn of the millennium. The eighteen greens on Palms have been remade to USGA specifications, as have one and eighteen on Pines. Lakes have been dug, mounds created by residue dirt, a hole shortened here and there. According to Dennis, Pines is easier, Palms now in better condition, and male members are no longer so fussy.

I toured Palms, the inner course. For the average golfer shooting in the nineties, Palms is the course to play. Some interesting holes include the penal par-3 sixth, a scenic green at the altered eighth, and a respectable trio of holes to finish the round. After an inspection of Pines, the difference was obvious. This is for the single-digit handicapper, the powerful player. An angry golfer would not like Pines—would get beaten up by the test, and most likely never return.

Pines number one is a par 4 of medium difficulty. As long as the tee shot gets away around the corner, it leaves a mid-iron approach. This position is also away and out of sight of the audience at the starter's hut.

Pines number two is a 161-yard par 3, parallel to the executive airport runway but unlike in surface. The mounded fairway runs to a smallish green lobed by deep bunkers. Time your swing right and your ball can have added sound effects and wind turbulence. The third curves in a lengthy left-handed manner beside a lake to a green of 2,300 square feet. A small pot bunker behind acts like the period to a sentence.

Palms on Palms number six.

Even a high handicapper should be able to clear the fairway bunker on the 340-yard fourth. A mid-iron or less remains to the target, which falls noticeably to the right. Five has a tree in the middle of the line of sight. Hit to the left of it to find the center of the fairway (see color plate 19).

Runways to the greens show the influence of Bruce Devlin rather than his erstwhile partner. Playing professionals cannot devote as much time to sites as they would wish. Sometimes their ideas can disappear in construction. Mr. Devlin readily admits his designs display a penchant for the bump-and-run shot. Studying their courses is akin to deducing whether a song was by Lennon or McCartney. Pines is a Devlin, while Colony West, for example, is more von Hagge; heavily bunkered, it requires the target golf that became the nationwide trend.

Eight, rated hardest hole, has two flashed bunkers behind the pin, for those taking too much joy in bumping and running. The turn is similar to some links courses in the British Isles, in that you can't get much farther from the clubhouse.

The tenth measures 543 yards, and only 14 yards of mown fairway separate two bunkers 280 yards from the target. Eleven has most difficult rating on this side; the green sheds in three directions from the center. The next two holes spoon each other in par-5, par-4 fashion, and are of similar difficulty.

Ray Frei, a volunteer course ranger and local golf nut, leads parties of forty or more to other courses around the state. He recited local opinion that "the back nine doesn't really begin until the thirteenth."

The closing holes start out in the woods and come back past road, mall, and purple-painted public utility station, into the southeasterly breeze. It reminded me of a chase sequence from a film. You dart into the tunnel of trees at fourteen; the green, deep and narrow, falls away to the right toward two greenside bunkers. A lone palm tree on one-shot fifteen's runway obscures the left half of the tiny target, which is bunkered to the right.

Sixteen slides around a lake for the final 200-yard stretch. The green is guarded on the right by bunkers front and rear. Seventeen, a 164-yard par 3, might require clubbing up playing into the prevailing wind. Water lies to the right, and trees opposite greatly assist in narrowing focus on the pin. The last has water to the left, a flash bunker at front left, and a green that disperses from a central crown.

Across the wooden bridge the clubhouse restaurant stands; the building could grace any Edward Hopper painting. Pompano Beach prompted a feeling the world hasn't changed much since the days of diners and jukeboxes. People come with sticks and balls to emulate their heroes in recreation. Here's hoping golf will roll back the years.

Colony West Country Club

6800 NW Avenue, Tamarac 33321
(954) 726-8430
www.colonywestcc.com

Green fee: $95

Architects: Robert von Hagge and Bruce Devlin, 1970
Par 71
Blue yardage 6,420; course rating 71.7; slope rating 135
White yardage 5,602; course rating 73.4; slope rating 137

*Directions: From I-95 exit 32, take 870 (Commercial Boulevard) west 7.5
miles. At NW 88th Avenue (Pine Island Road) turn right (north). In 0.9 miles,
entrance is on right.*

*From 91 (Florida's Turnpike) exit 62, take 870 (Commercial Boulevard) west
3.5 miles. At NW 88th Avenue (Pine Island Road) turn right (north). In 0.9
miles, entrance is on right.*

*From 869 (Sawgrass Expressway) exit 3, take 870 (Commercial Boulevard)
east 1.7 miles. At NW 88th Avenue (Pine Island Road) turn left (north). In 0.9
miles, entrance is on right.*

Mannerism was a style of painting in the sixteenth century. Figures were shown
bursting out of the frame as though they were just entering or leaving the can-
vas. All was monumental and overwhelming. Perhaps Robert von Hagge and
Bruce Devlin adopted the style of Rosso and Bronzino as a theme for Colony
West. My first impression was a few long holes scattered about a residential
area of pink condominiums. I read that Jack Nicklaus had said the course was
too difficult. On my second visit I became enthralled with the 6,420-yard monster of Devlin and von Hagge. ("The Count," as he is called in the profession,
is known to arrive at construction sites attired in knickers and a gold lamé
cape.)

The lack of a driving range shows there's no better preparation for the round
than the hardest hole, a par 5 of 570 yards. I'm sure many would accept a 6 on
the card and move immediately to number two. To the right a pair of mounded

Down the chute
on six.

fairway bunkers won't cure your slice, more likely accentuate it; water on the
left will attract a pull. A wide green gently sloping left should settle jangled
nerves.

On the third, a conspicuous mound at the left side of the fairway is the best
marker for the approach. It leaves 175 yards to a target with a narrow entrance
and bunkers on both sides. Average-sized for greens at Colony West, this is 35
yards deep and half that in width.

Luckily, the carts have GPS systems, as the next hole is across a road. A common mistake is to head for the adjacent par-3 eighth; well, it fooled me anyway.
You'll cross road between green and tee six times in your round.

Four's fairway elbows right, and second shots require a draw to take advantage of the receptive, angled green. This curls back right to double as the green of hole six. The 167-yard fifth shares a runway tee box with the 510-yard seventh. Five's one-shot green falls away to its unprotected side, on the right.

A chute of trees borders the sixth fairway until it angles right at the landing area. Entrance to the green is from the air only; bunkers crouch crablike around the target. The seventh winds around the lake shared with the fourth. An optical mound, fronting the target to the left, hides the final 40 yards of fairway.

Across the road a heavily bunkered green calls for precision in a tee shot of 180 yards. The outward nine steams back to the clubhouse. Fairway bunkers lie at driving distance. Greenside bunkers bolster a putting surface full of subtle breaks.

Ten and eleven provide a breather, par 4s averaging 360 yards. Although the former requires aerial approach, as at the third, a mound to the left of the fairway can aid in getting airborne.

The Infamous Twelfth is the hole that bit back at Jack. Mr. Nicklaus once took 7 here. Rated hardest hole on this side, it measures 411 yards. The tee shot

The Infamous Twelfth.

is to the angle of a dogleg. Going left, the second shot plays through a tree-lined corridor and over water to an open, flat green.

The next tee box is shaped like a boomerang, from the thirteenth curving back to become the sixteenth tee. Twelve and seventeen also share a tee box; theirs is T-shaped. Despite this economy in usage, Colony West covers some 175 acres.

Hole fourteen is another lanky child, 509 yards, with water along the right. Not the most scenic hole, it needs loft to reach a well-bunkered target. A word of caution: where an occasional opening for a bump-and-run shot looks likely, the runways are lush and watered on most days, resulting in bump and stop. Even the shortest, easiest hole, the 140-yard seventeenth, leaves no choice but aerial assault.

The broad final fairway calls for more sky to reach the clubhouse green—a last flourish by the Count. You can imagine him turning on his heel and striding away triumphantly, his cape swirling as he goes. A half-hidden sign, perhaps Bruce Devlin's ironic apology, reads "Thanks For Playing Colony West." Their working partnership was by some accounts enthusiastically heated. Neither would let it be, with daily clashes before compromise. To have lasted fourteen years in association shows how creative was their chemistry.

Bruce Devlin left the partnership in 1987 to prepare for the Champions Tour. He continues to design courses internationally from his home in the Southwest. The Devlin course at St. Andrews, Scotland, is a notable addition; another in his native Australia was under construction at the time of writing.

Robert von Hagge has run his own team of design associates for nearly twenty years. He operates out of Texas.

Colony West was intended to be a venue for the Honda Classic on the PGA Tour, but was never included. The nines were reversed and the tenth (the old number one) shortened when the clubhouse was built, which lowered par to 71 and which explains why the first is now the hardest hole. The owner briefed the architects to create a course that serious golfers could sink their teeth into. It's hard to believe fifty-two bunkers were removed from the original design before opening.

The course has staged minitour events and a television commercial with Chi Chi Rodriguez, and has the unique distinction of being the only public course Joe DiMaggio ever played. Although the tournament course record is 63, staff member Marty Stanovich has scored 62 on three separate occasions, and one of those included a bogey. I think he should find somewhere more difficult to play.

Miami Beach Golf Club

2301 Alton Road, Miami Beach 33140
(305) 532-3350
www.miamibeachgolfclub.com

Green fee: $185

Architect: Arthur Hills, 2002
Par 72
Blue yardage 6,430; course rating 71.1; slope rating 128
Red yardage 5,039; course rating 70.1; slope rating 124

*Directions: From I-95 exit 4B, take I-195 east 3.6 miles to exit 5 South onto
route 907 (Alton Road). Entrance is on left in 0.8 miles.*

*From Venetian Causeway/Dade Boulevard, turn left at 907 (Alton Road) and
go 0.6 miles; entrance is on right.*

Reopening in 2002 after an eighteen-month masterful overhaul by Arthur
Hills, this is an appealing entree on the South Beach recreational menu. The
course was known as Bayshore when Robert von Hagge and Bruce Devlin re-
designed it in the early 1970s, but a scorecard from 1919 recently found on eBay
reveals Miami Beach Golf Club as the earliest moniker. Stories from the 1920s
have U.S. senators sharing the clubhouse dining room with mobsters like Al
Capone—golf proving, as ever, a great leveler. In its Bayshore days, the course
played host to PGA Tour events, one notable winner being Gary Player, and to
Shell's Wonderful World of Golf series.

Today the club promotes a private experience in a public setting with argu-
ably the most glamorous nineteenth hole in existence, South Beach. A new
clubhouse in chic art-deco style, eight-minute intervals between tee times,
superior range balls, and a chance to rub shoulders with stars of hoops and
Hollywood do not come cheap. Forty thousand rounds of golf are played here
annually. Memberships will be capped at around two hundred, half the number
of resident iguanas. The $7 million renovation has the management hopeful of
at least a national amateur championship in the future.

Remodeling the golf course was a major undertaking. Altogether 90,000 cubic yards of earth were moved from the lakes to create mounding, leaving 30 acres of water, 100 acres of land, 3 acres of tees, 3 acres of greens, and 2.5 acres of sand. The biggest winner at Miami Beach in recent times is Paspalum grass. It covers the whole course from tees to greens and is salt water tolerant. Brought from West Africa on slave ships, Paspalum was used as bedding in the hold for the unfortunates. When the slaves were disembarked in Virginia and the Carolinas, the grass was dropped overboard into the marshlands and took root.

Research by Dr. Ron Duncan of the University of Georgia has found a twenty-first-century use for the grass. Ocean water contains salt at 35,000 parts per million. Diluted to 17,000 parts per million, it can be used through the green areas for irrigation. To prevent salt accumulation, the figure is decreased to an optimum level of two parts fresh to one part salt water. Paspalum is very hardy and discourages fungus growth, thus minimizing the need for fertilizer. Miami Beach is the first public facility in the east to be entirely Paspalum. It is tempting to speculate that one day all coastal courses will be so efficient. The grass, however, cannot thrive in cold weather.

Ten's green complex with number one in the background.

South Beach on the seventeenth.

The front half includes three par 3s and plays 500 yards shorter than the back. Holes eight through thirteen are the toughest stretch. For the par-5 start, bunkers sit to the left 275 yards out from an elevated target. The second, a short par 4, angles left to a forward-sloping green 40 yards deep.

Three, a one-shot of 153 yards, has water on the right and a pot bunker left. The architect's advice is to hit to the right side; a bailout area at rear left is the best place to miss the green. Four is a real test of par. Fading the tee shot around the corner leaves 175 yards to the pin; the right side of the green is mounded, and the putting surface falls to right center.

The par-5 fifth requires a drive of 250 yards to clear cross bunkers at fairway right. The second shot must also clear greenside hazards. The target falls away to the front left quarter. Six is a par 3 with a greenside hazard to the right. Personally, I rate it the easiest hole on the course, it being 50 yards shorter than the seventeenth and not as fiercely guarded.

Seventy yards of staggered sand at the seventh have the fairway corkscrewing on approach to a green tilting left and bunkered right. At the 353-yard eighth, either you drive over the cross bunker to the right, or water forces a carry to get home. The green leans right into its attendant horseshoe bunker.

The par-3 ninth returns to the clubhouse, 203 yards from the blues and only 170 yards from the white tees.

The tenth is a great hole for the strategist, a par 5 with bunkers at both landing areas. Big hitters will go for the pin with their second shot. A raised green and prevailing wind from the right must be taken into account. When played as a three-shot hole, the second landing area is narrow; water lies to the left, and a trio of pot bunkers cover entrance to the green.

Twelve is a 550-yard par 5 with a dazzling waste area that must cover a quarter of an acre. Water provides the second hazard on this hole. Once again the landing area narrows as it advances to the green. Lay up to favored iron length for the approach.

Holes fifteen through seventeen are the climactic movement of the Arthur Hills Miami Beach variations. Fifteen is the third par 5 of more than 500 yards on this nine. From the fairway bunker, the ground rises to a mounded, sloping, bunkered green. A false front deceives the eye, so clubbing up is the sensible option.

Some of the more primal players will attempt to drive sixteen's 323 yards. Water is more intrusive than before, making the fairway slide to the right. For those playing a more rhythmical approach, the green sits between two bunkers poised to clash like cymbals if your ball quavers.

The glorious seventeenth is moated by water and surrounded by sand. From rear left the green falls toward the tee. Jim Torba, course superintendent at the time of my visit, said club selection for 158 yards is anything from 7-iron to 4-wood, depending how strong the wind blows. The par-4 finish strays little from the straight and narrow. A quiet 400-yard chord resolves this eighteen-hole symphony.

Crandon Golf Course

6700 Crandon Boulevard, Key Biscayne 33149
(305) 361-9129
www.co.miami-dade.fl.us/parks/golf.asp

Green fee: $148

Architects: Robert von Hagge and Bruce Devlin, 1972
Par 72(Blue)/73(Gold)
Blue yardage 6,842; course rating 74.1; slope rating 143
Gold yardage 5,423; course rating 71.8; slope rating 130

Directions: Crandon is on Key Biscayne. From I-95 South exit 1, take the Rick-enbacker Causeway; 5.3 miles after the toll plaza, entrance is on right.

This was my first adventure around a golf course in a ranger's cart. The ranger was initially reluctant to entertain a stranger. By the end of the afternoon we were swapping jokes, business cards, and cold refreshments in Crandon's muscular new clubhouse. George Fisher, in his senior years, has the enthusiasm of a teenager. Born and bred in Miami, he has seen the city go in and out of fashion and come full circle. He remembers when it was one of the best-kept secrets in the Southeast. All that changed in 1960 with Castro and the influx of Cubans, as the city's economy intertwined with expatriated funds. The local Latino culture stems from this tide. George Fisher credits Richard Nixon with Crandon Golf Course. My face wrinkles with questioning disdain. "Sure it was his idea," says George. "He had a house here on Key Biscayne."

Although Crandon's opening is contemporary with the former president, the layout is the brainchild of Robert von Hagge and Bruce Devlin. Students of this pairing of architects will know they do not shy away from length, especially on par 5s. Crandon's opener is no exception. Mangrove trees line the left side, and low handicappers should attempt a drive over the corner at this dogleg. The landing area is broad, but bunkered to the right. Played as a three-shot hole, placement left of the second landing area's set of hazards leaves a wedge to the slightly elevated green. The next hole also doglegs left along an alley of mangroves. The green is ridged at the left and slopes away to the right-hand side. Crandon's greens are on the fast side, perhaps contributing to the pace of play. George hints it's not unusual for a round to take five hours.

The third is 182 yards, carried over swamp and front bunkers to the small target. Four is a mammoth 616 yards, measuring 600 yards even from the white tees; not many will reach this in two. The fifth has some pleasing definition with mounding to the left. The green, surrounded by bunkers, warps from rear left to front right. George pauses to show me a fairway bunker on the right, 130 yards from the flag. "Five years ago, eight-iron from here into the hole. I eagled it!" He beams.

He neglects to say how he scored on number six, a par 3 of 180 yards. Bunkers are strategically placed front, right, and rear, and water guards the entire left side. The putting surface tilts to the left at the front, but to the right at the back.

The seventh is one of the world's great golf holes. A wall of mangroves blocks the right side of the fairway. No matter where the ball lands at the apex of the 415-yard dogleg, the player is faced with a carry over water to the green. I was baffled about how to get home; the chicken in me opted for the pitch-and-wedge approach. An ibis turned its head as if refusing to acknowledge the presence of domestic fowl.

Here be crocodiles.

Number eight is a backyard bunt, a 144-yard one-shot, and the easiest on the course. I'm tempted to think it was added as an afterthought: "I say, Robert, we've only got seventeen holes here!" "By Jove, Bruce, you're right! Better stick another one in over there." (You can tell I'm no stranger to design conferences.)

George regales me with stories of visiting politicians and celebrities. Rudy Giuliani has played here, and this course-with-no-members sees a more frequent visitor in the current governor. State business aside, once a month he plays his favorite track.

The back nine is more open and a good drive longer. The tenth plays as a double dogleg, two sections of fairway connected by a chad of land merely 13 yards wide. The broad green is shallow and slopes forward into a front bunker.

The eleventh is supposedly Crandon's hardest, although George would hand that distinction to the chicken-picking seventh. For the big hitter, the fairway narrows drastically: bunkers to the left, trees and water to the right. The green's left side is hipped by mounds and falls away rapidly to the front right.

Twelve is a picture postcard hole, a mid-iron over water to a wide but shallow dance floor chaperoned behind by two beefy bunkers. Don't try to retrieve

Miami skyline.

balls lost in the water—here be crocodiles. George tells a gruesome tale at the fifteenth. One Saturday morning, while his threesome waited to hit their approaches to the narrow-mouthed green, an adult green iguana plopped into the lake. A basking crocodile slipped into the water on the other side and homed in like a torpedo upon its prey. George estimates the croc lifted itself four feet out of the water with the helpless iguana writhing in its jaws. It's enough to put you off your backswing.

The final tee box is longer than the eighth hole entirely; it's longer than the twelfth from the whites; in fact, it measures more than any of the par 3s from the forward tees. A gap in the trees halfway down the fairway affords a stunning view of Miami's mainland skyline.

George ducks in and out of the mangroves collecting balls; he's been doing this all the way. He says half of them are his anyway.

Crandon's scorecard proclaims it "one of the top public courses in the world . . . on the only subtropical lagoon in North America." The Royal Caribbean Classic, a Senior PGA Tour event, is held here every year. Past winners include Lee Trevino (twice), Gary Player, Larry Nelson, and Bruce Fleischer, who in 2004 captured his third title. Stars by the dozen, but for me Crandon's star will always be George Fisher. Bless you, George.

The Biltmore

1210 Anastasia Avenue, Coral Gables 33134
(305) 460-5364
www.biltmorehotel.com

Green fee: $150

Architect: Donald Ross, 1925
Par 71 (white), 73 (red)
White yardage 6,265; course rating 70.0; slope rating 123
Red yardage 5,773; course rating 73.4; slope rating 123

Directions: From US 1 in Coral Gables, take Grenada Boulevard 1.1 miles. Cross Bird Road and continue 0.5 miles. At Anastasia Avenue turn left; entrance is on left in 0.3 miles.

At the Biltmore, the imposing hotel looms over the golf, figuratively speaking. Since the hotel is south facing, realistically its shadow hardly troubles the course at all. Inside one would expect to find a salon full of characters from a Poirot or Miss Marple drama, period dress and pince-nez. The haughty scrutiny one would expect from a grande dame of such age need not necessarily be reflected in the pro-shop staff, but then again, I'm sure some guests relish the whipping.

Donald Ross, the course architect of 1925, looks rather benign in those familiar photographs. The Biltmore—the golf course, that is—at first glance seems a light-fingered recreational diversion for hotel guests and not meant to thieve them of their golfing egos and manicured handicaps. Closer inspection reveals skullduggery afoot. The course has robbed many of their pride and dignity: flappers and floozies and plus-four-wearing Woosters, cigar-smoking Brewsters and honking snowbirds. And it is abundantly clear, ladies and gentlemen, that the architect did it. His fingerprints are all over the course.

Land developer George Merrick had a vision of making Coral Gables "the City Beautiful" and persuaded John McEntee Bowman, the Biltmore magnate, to build a hotel to "serve as a center of sports and fashion." From the great hotel's beginnings it was clear all was to be superlative; travertine floors, marble columns, mahogany furnishings, and hand-painted frescoes. The centerpiece is a 93-foot tower modeled after Seville's Giralda, built as the minaret of a Moorish mosque and later to become the bell tower of the cathedral reputed to be the final resting place of Christopher Columbus.

The hotel opened in 1926 and became a showpiece of the jazz age. Royalty and celebrities dined and danced or took a dip in the largest hotel pool in the United States. Johnny Weissmuller was swimming instructor here before his Tarzan days in Hollywood.

Swinging off at the first, don't go into the trees on this side's only par 5. The second is a 160-yard par 3; two oval bunkers guard the green. Three and four are par 4s sharing length and ease, and so far it's been a stroll in the park.

The next three toughen up the whole deal. Strong players will easily clear fairway bunkers at the fifth; shorter hitters must contend with these hazards and more placed greenside. The tee shot at six plays to a narrowing landing area. Trees to the right mark 175 yards to the flag. Water runs diagonally from the left across the front of the well-bunkered green. The seventh doglegs left with the same water affecting the approach.

The GPS system in the cart advises landing on the left of the fairway at the ninth. My two cents' worth is to play to the right, taking out an enormous bun-

The grande dame.

ker to the left of the green. Attack the pin from below, as the putting surface is built into a mound and pitches forward steeply.

Ten is a straight par 4. Love-handle mounds squeeze the fairway to 15 yards at wedge distance, inviting a bump and run into the open green. Two left-angled doglegs follow. Eleven's green is set back further than it appears from the apex—again, do I need better glasses? Come and see for yourself. The twelfth is a charming hole of 355 yards. Draped like spaniels' ears, bunkers protrude from the front of the green for 30 yards.

Thirteen is yet another hole shaped to the left. Two huge bunkers support the elongated green. Combined, they must be larger than the green itself. The fourteenth is a one-shot hole played over water to a forward-sloping surface with a bunker to the right.

Fifteen is the hardest hole on this nine. Walking to the landing area, there seems no safe way in. It plays as a par 5 from the forward tees. The high handicapper also would do well treating this as a three-shot hole. Remember, bogey was considered respectable in our great-grandfather's day. How many of us have admitted verbally a willingness to settle for bogey golf and no worse? The same way a scratch golfer will wish for consistent par—"and maybe I'll get lucky today." The same way a pro thinks: "Birdie fest—and maybe I'll get lucky today."

Seventeen is the longest hole at 515 yards. Eventually one finds the green guarded by water and winged by sand. Finally, a hole shaped to the right. Bunkers and mounds force placement on the left of the fairway. The narrow green is lightly bunkered.

Following in the footsteps of Walter Hagen and Gene Sarazen from the hotel's heyday, you are also preceding stars of the future. The world's largest youth sports and arts festival, the Junior Orange Bowl International, is held in Coral Gables from October to December. In recent years the golf championship has seen such winners as Tiger Woods, Sergio Garcia, and Grace Park. This concours d'élégance would not be out of place on the Mediterranean Riviera. The Biltmore is a four-star hotel with course attached, rather than a course with accompanying hotel. You visit for grandeur as much as for golf (see color plate 20).

The Biltmore Hotel's exclusive elevator to the fifteenth floor might be the last ride for the perfectionist hoping to conquer from the air the eighteen holes that proved his undoing at ground level. Did he fall, or was he pushed?

Palmetto Golf Course

9300 SW 152nd Street, Miami 33157
(305) 235-1069
www.co.miami-dade.fl.us/parks/golf.asp

Green fee: $40 (walking $18)

Architect: Dick Wilson, 1959
Par 70 (blue) / 73 (red)
Blue yardage 6,648; course rating 72.2; slope rating 128
Red yardage 5,710; course rating 73.4; slope rating 125

Directions: The course is situated at the corner of US1 and SW 152nd Street (Coral Reef Drive). From US 1, turn west on SW 152nd Street and go 0.2 miles; entrance is on left.

From 821 (Florida's Turnpike), exit 16, go east on 992 (SW 152nd Street) 2.2 miles; entrance is on right.

Looking for a bit of golf history in Miami without it costing three figures? Driving past from the Turnpike, Palmetto looked like a typical Florida flat-track municipal. On closer inspection, it turns out to be a county-owned course dating back to 1959 and a Dick Wilson design. Built two years before his infamous Blue Monster of Doral, this is two points shy of its younger brother in the slope rating but a tall order at 6,648 yards in length.

The Palmetto Country Club folded in the early 1960s and since then the Department of Parks and Recreation of Miami-Dade County has run the course. The old clubhouse burned to the ground on New Year's Day 1990—a stray firework, perhaps—and the new clubhouse, pleasantly italianate in architecture, was unveiled nine years later. Hurricane Andrew uprooted many established trees, but some were quickly set upright again, reasserting the traditional feel of the place with their maturity. Pink shower trees, bridalveil, and yellow tubebuia are recent memorial additions.

Erik Compton, the Nationwide and PGA Tour professional, learned his game on this course. The winner of the annual Dade County Youth Fair, played at Palmetto, receives an automatic invitation to the Junior Orange Bowl International Championship held at the Biltmore.

Palms line the rear of the fifth green.

However simple Palmetto may appear at first glance, every hole has at least two greenside bunkers, and the majority have four. A bag containing lost clubs stands in manager Susan Walker's office. In it I spotted a 3-wood and a putter; the rest were wedges. The sands of time make us all forgetful, the sands at Palmetto evidently more so.

Appropriately, the first fairway runs through an avenue of palmettos. A pot bunker to the right leaves 250 yards to the target. A canal, 50 yards wide, will be crossed ten times during the round. Two flashed bunkers lie to the right; the green is tucked away left and guarded by sand at the front.

Number two runs back parallel to the first, and the next completes the three-hole corridor. This is the only stretch where one feels an up-and-down effect, once described to me as Interstate golf. For all that, they are also two of the hardest holes. The second is a straightaway par 4 of 430 yards, the third longer by a few strides. A well-placed 250-yard tee shot leaves 175 yards to the elevated, heavily bunkered target. Did I forget to mention the canal? It cuts a swath across the fairway just short of the green.

The fourth measures 319 yards and doglegs right to a raised green, its bunkers whorled like the petals of a flower. The green slopes from rear left and gathers to right center. Next, a 187-yard par 3 has a teardrop green resembling an alien skull. Backed by a row of palm trees, the putting table is 25 yards deep, 17 yards wide at the rear, and only half that width at the front. The runway entrance is narrower still.

Seven is a heroic one-shot over two bodies of water with bunkers at the front and a large collection bunker behind. The shallow green slopes from left to right.

At 405 yards the eighth seems a gift for the long hitter, but a 300-yard drive will end up in the canal. A layup to favored mid- or short iron length is the wise play. On number nine, water lies near the tee box, the fairway bows slightly right, and bunkers are placed 100 yards out. The elevated green has a backdrop of palms. Downstage three finger bunkers point down the fairway; clubbing up on the approach is a good move.

The back nine opens with two easier holes, but twelve is the one to beat on this side. Four bunkers lie at the landing area, and more pepper the entrance to the green from 95 yards in. Thirteen's green is tucked left, favoring a little draw on the approach.

The next pair feature our friend the canal, cutting off green and tee respectively. A mid-handicapper needs a long iron to reach the green on the fourteenth. Fifteen, 399 yards long, doglegs right, and an aiming bunker at the

The pleasantly italianate clubhouse.

outer angle leaves 150 yards to the target. Three sand hazards wait on the inside for unsuccessful attempts to cut the corner. The green is impossible to access along the ground. A pot bunker in front is receptive as a catcher's glove; two companion mitts behind will round up any overenthusiastic aerial attack.

There's respite for the bump and run at the sixteenth. The welcoming green is one of the larger putting surfaces. A horseshoe of sand rings the rear. Bunkers fortify the par-3 seventeenth; a thin strip of narrow green protrudes at the front. Is this hole sticking its tongue out at us? A classic par 4 finishes the round. A drive over the canal one last time, and along a processional avenue of trees to the raised green, bunkered at every corner.

Have you wondered why professionals achieve such longevity? Walking four miles a day, six times a week, twenty-six weeks a year for the best part of fifty years might have something to do with it. Many courses in recent years are designed as mandatory cart tracks: longer distances between greens and tees, pace of play, and increased revenue are all part of the picture. The club flyer entices you to come "play the game the way it was meant to be played . . . Walk Palmetto."

60

Key West Golf Club

6450 College Road, Key West 33040
(305) 294-5232
www.keywestgolf.com

Green fee: $177

Architect: Rees Jones, 1983
Par 70
Blue yardage 6,512; course rating 71.2; slope rating 124
Red yardage 5,003; course rating 70.1; slope rating 118

*Directions: From Miami, take US 1 south 154 miles and turn right on College
Road, Stock Island. In 0.5 miles, entrance is on right.*

Heard of the restaurant at the end of the universe? Well, this is the golf course
at the end of North America, at the southern extremity of the United States.
It's a long way to go for a game of golf, I grant you, but special for those who
want to say they've played in that geographical location. It's not really on Key
West. Stock Island is the key immediately north, so you could say it's the key
to Key West.

The local U.S. Navy base constructed the original nine-hole routing, and Er-
nest Hemingway is known to have stalked these fairways. One resident remembers when fairways were coral rock and players brought their own Astroturf
or clump of sod to hit from. In 1983, the miraculous Charles "Sonny" McCoy
enticed Rees Jones to extend the course to the full eighteen holes. McCoy, a
third generation "conch" and currently a Monroe County commissioner, was
the five-time mayor of Key West who rescued the city from bankruptcy. In
addition to playing a key part in the 1980 Mariel boatlift of 125,000 Cubans
to Florida, McCoy on September 10, 1978, using only one board, water-skied
nonstop from Key West to Havana in six hours and ten minutes.

A bronze bust of the real McCoy stands rightfully by the first tee. Painted
coconuts serve as tee box markers and add an amusing touch. A large mounded
bunker, 200 yards from the tee, must be cleared to leave a mid-iron to a green
with subtle folds and breaks. Two has mounded cloverleaf bunkers on both

sides of the forward-sloping green. Returning parallel, the third hole is of similar length and difficulty; a deep pot bunker sits to the right of the target.

Four and five are played through sea grape trees, whose leaves are used farther south in the Caribbean as makeshift plates at picnics and beach parties. After the hazard on the angle of the slight dogleg is avoided, the flat fourth green sits tucked in a corner and bunkered on three sides. The fifth is supposedly easy: 161 yards, with water in front, deep bunkers on both sides and the generous putting surface leaning to the right. Tricky is a better description.

Six is the strongest hole on the card, a 434-yard dogleg right. With water off the tee and running right, a maximum carry will leave as little as 200 yards to the pin. The guarded green slides away to rear left.

Mangroves line the fairway on number seven, which kinks left from 150 yards out. The eighth is called the Mangrove Hole, 178 yards all the way over mangroves. Invisible from the tee is the sanded smiley segment ringing the green at the front. A sizeable bunker lies behind as well, and a central ridge in the putting surface disperses balls left or right. Bunkers define the angle of the fairway at the ninth. The green undulates formidably, balked at the left by a wall of sand.

Book a tee time for tomorrow.

The home stretch.

The workings of the club are compact yet all embracing. A small clubhouse contains a large dining facility and an ample bar to rival any on storied Duval Street. Adjacent stands an enclosed driving range of sufficient size to house a small family of wild animals. The carts are fed and watered in a shed worthy of any New England dairy barn. Young Matt Harris helped me in the pro shop. The younger of two brothers, he's considered the black sheep of the family because he chose golf over fishing.

An attraction of opposites begins the back nine. Starting with a dogleg left, mounded bunkers shape the outer angle. The green accepts a bump and run, but its centerfold ridge sheds balls like water, and the rear is framed by sand. The eleventh spoons back on its partner, favoring a fade off the tee. This green's bumps and hollows draw everything to the center; bunkers the shape of jigsaw pieces sit on both sides.

An easier trio follow. Twelve is a mere drive of 362 yards for the extreme hitter. For the rest of us, water lines the fairway's left, while a bunker to the right guards the approach. Following a 188-yard par 3, US 1 runs alongside fourteen's open fairway. The raised putting surface, seemingly circled by sand, has a tiny way in from the right.

Fifteen doglegs left with a steep-faced bunker defining the apex, 150 yards from the pin. Trim housing lines the right of the fairway; homes are visible on a handful of holes and are alluring rather than intrusive. Since space is at a premium on the keys, I wasn't tempted to inquire into real estate prices.

Sixteen is prettiest of the par 3s, played over water with a three-lobed bunker sitting below the green. The seventeenth doglegs right, with mounding at one side and bunkers on the other. Cavernous bunkers bolster the green. A sign en route to the eighteenth tee informs us that "Same Day Replays" are available, "Pay Cart Fee Only." The early-bird advantage reaps dividends. Knolls and hollows run right for the length of the home fairway. The clubhouse looks very welcoming indeed from here.

You pay top dollar at Key West Golf Club; the twilight fees in high season are what you'd expect to shell out for a richly manicured track on the mainland. The laws of supply and demand ring most true in small, remote locations. If you leave your clubs at home, expect to hand over $40 for a top-of-the-line rental set. No sense being a grouch, show them the money. Hit, hope, and have fun.

Local residents relish their Saturday morning scramble. They refer to toffee-nosed northerners, who haven't thawed out yet, as "not Key Westersized." I expect this involves a cocktail on Duval Street, a lot of deep-sea fishing, and the odd round of golf.

You're now faced with a choice: return to the Frozen North or book a tee time for tomorrow.

Selected Bibliography

I list here only the main works used in preparation of *Florida's Fairways*. This is not a complete record of all sources of data. Libraries and museums provided a wealth of information and references regarding local history. Online search engines were also used to access material. The story of Ernie Sabayrac (Falcon's Fire) was an exhibit in *The Florida Swing* in early 2005 at Orlando's History Center.

Two works that aided in the initial selection of courses:
Golf Digest's Places to Play. 5th ed. New York: Fodor's, 2002.
www.thegolfcourses.net/

Two works to which I referred constantly:
Cornish, Geoffrey S., and Ronald E. Whitten. *The Architects of Golf: A Survey of Golf Course Design from Its Beginnings to the Present, with an Encyclopedic Listing of Golf Course Architects and Their Courses.* Rev. ed. of *The Golf Course.* New York: HarperCollins, 1993.
Graves, Robert Muir, and Geoffrey S. Cornish. *Golf Course Design.* New York: John Wiley and Sons, 1998.

Two works that provide a perfect introduction for the armchair golf architect:
Doak, Tom. *The Anatomy of a Golf Course: The Art of Golf Architecture.* Short Hills, N.J.: Burford Books, 1992.
Shackelford, Geoff. *Grounds for Golf: The History and Fundamentals of Golf Course Design.* New York: Thomas Dunne Books, St. Martin's Press, 2003.

Two works found in pro shops:
Hills, Arthur. *The Works of Art: Golf Course Designs by Arthur Hills.* With Michael Patrick Shiels. Virginia Beach: Donning, 2004.
Tillinghast, A. W. *Gleanings from the Wayside: My Recollections as a Golf Architect.* Edited by Richard C. Wolffe, Robert S. Trebus, and Stuart F. Wolffe. Short Hills, N.J.: TreeWolf Productions, 2001.

Two works that proved valuable in ornithological and arboreal identification:

Kale, Herbert W., II, and David S. Mehr. *Florida's Birds: A Handbook and Reference*. Illustrated by Karl Karalus. Sarasota: Pineapple Press, 1990.

Williams, Winston. *Florida's Fabulous Trees: Their Stories*. 2nd ed. Tampa: World Publications, 1998.

Finally, the book that rekindled my obsession with golf, opened my mind to golf course construction, and drew me to Florida:

Strawn, John. *Driving the Green: The Making of a Golf Course*. New York: HarperCollins, 1991.

Alan K. Moore is a British-born American citizen who, after twenty years as a tour guide, has turned to writing. His first book, *Adventure Guide to Grenada, St. Vincent and the Grenadines*, coauthored with his wife, Cindy Kilgore, was named Best Guide Book of 2004 by the Caribbean Tourism Organization. He lives in the Frozen North. He may be reached at www.floridasfairways.com.